THE REAL READER'S QU

Slightly Foxed

'A Familiar Country'

NO.78   SUMMER 2023

Editors: Gail Pirkis & Hazel Wood
Marketing & publicity: Steph Allen, Jennie Harrison Bunning & Hattie Summers
Subscriptions, orders & bookshops: Jess Dalby & Jemima Ratcliffe

Cover illustration: Ron Kingswood, *Wheat Field,* oil on canvas

Ron Kingswood incorporates his love of nature with a highly subjective approach, conjuring painterly brushwork and inventive compositions with his desire to convey the extraordinary power and beauty of colour. He studied at H. B. Beal in London, Ontario, and received a degree in Bird Ecology and Ornithology at the University of Western Ontario. He has exhibited internationally in both private and public galleries, and his work is included in many public collections, in both Canada and the USA. He now lives and works in Sparta, Ontario. To see more of his work, visit www.jonathancooper.co.uk.

Back cover fox by James Nunn
Design by Octavius Murray
Layout by Andrew Evans
Colophon and tailpiece by David Eccles

Published by Slightly Foxed Limited
53 Hoxton Square
London N1 6PB

tel 020 7033 0258
email office@foxedquarterly.com
www.foxedquarterly.com

Slightly Foxed is published quarterly in early March, June, September and December

Annual subscription rates (4 issues)
UK and Ireland £56; Overseas £64

Single copies of this issue can be bought for £14.50 (UK) or £16.50 (Overseas)

All back issues in printed form are also available

ISBN 978-1-910898-80-2

ISSN 1742-5794

Printed and bound by Smith Settle, Yeadon, West Yorkshire

Contents

Contents

Isla Middleton

From the Editors

The past few months have seen some significant comings and goings at *Slightly Foxed*. Sadly, we said goodbye to Anna (or rather *au revoir* – once a fox always a fox) who understandably felt it was time for a change after being with us for nearly fourteen years. Many of you will have spoken to Anna, who was loved by everyone for her kindness and her can-do attitude, and admired for her wide reading and literary taste, which she often shared on the podcast. Nothing was too much trouble for her, and we're really going to miss her. Fortunately we still have lovely and super-hardworking Hattie and Jess who keep the office wheels on track and support Steph, who oversees our marketing and publicity; Aimi, who deals with financial mysteries such as the payroll and keeps us all calm; and Jemima, who joined as an intern and was such a success we asked her to stay. And a further bit of good news – Jennie, whose creative spark did so much in the early years to make *Slightly Foxed* what it is, is now back from maternity leave and turning her thoughts from small people to our design and marketing.

So we're going into the summer with a full team, not forgetting the dogs of course: Dusty who travels in daily with Jess and has become the de facto office dog; Jennie's Tarka and Griff; Maggie, Gideon and Humphrey, who keep tabs on Steph down in Sussex; and of course Gail's Stanley, who throws his weight about a bit (literally) when he comes up from Devon, and Chudleigh, the Grand Old Man, still benign, but in failing health and now becoming a little vague.

This summer's Slightly Foxed Edition is an intriguing memoir by an intriguing author. As a child in the 1960s Luke Jennings – now dance critic of the *Observer* and also the author of the *Killing Eve* trilogy – was fascinated by the mysterious depths of the lakes and rivers around his Sussex home. In *Blood Knots* (see p.13) he describes how his passion for fly-fishing gradually took hold, encouraged by his two boyhood heroes – his father, who had been awarded the Military Cross for bravery during the war, when he was badly burned, and Robert Nairac, a charismatic figure who first befriended him as a teacher at his prep school and who met his end when he was tortured and murdered by the IRA. The blood knot of the title is a knot used by fishermen, but this subtle and beautifully written book, as the words suggest, is about a great deal more than fishing.

And finally, to the 2022 *Slightly Foxed* Writers' competition. We had a number of interesting entries, but the two that stood out for their originality and the quality of their writing were Richard Brown's piece on Italo Calvino's *Invisible Cities* and Samuel Saloway-Cooke's on Edwin A. Abbott's *Flatland*. We really couldn't choose between them so we're happy to announce them as equal winners. Their pieces will appear in this year's autumn and winter issues respectively. Our thanks to everyone who entered, and congratulations to them both.

GAIL PIRKIS & HAZEL WOOD

A Familiar Country

FLORA WATKINS

In a cardboard box I put the essential objects we would need in our rented cottage, until we got the keys to our new house in Norfolk: my infant daughter's stuffed monkey, some paperwork, Cash's name tapes for the boys' new schools and the books we were reading at bedtime – *Five on a Treasure Island* for the boys, and for me my mother's tatty copy of *The Go-Between*, a still of Julie Christie from the film on the cover, which would date it to around 1971.

How fitting, I thought, as I secured some of its loose pages, that a book concerned with memory and impression and the long shadow cast by childhood experiences should be the one I reached for as we embarked on a new life away from London. As with the grown-up Leo, 'sixty-odd' at the start of the book, coming upon his old diary documenting his fateful visit to Brandham Hall in Norfolk in the summer of 1900, 'something came and went between us: the intimate pleasure of recognition, the almost mystical thrill of early ownership'.

In many ways, it was a strange book to bequeath to me, along with the more usual novels handed down from mother to daughter – *Rebecca*, *Invitation to the Waltz* – concerned as it is with the destruction of a little boy. The older Leo regards the diary with self-pity and self-reproach:

> had it not been for the diary, or what the diary stood for, everything would be different. I should not be sitting in this

L. P. Hartley, *The Go-Between* (1953)
Penguin · Pb · 336pp · £8.99 · ISBN 9780141187785

drab, flowerless room, where the curtains were not even drawn to hide the cold rain beating on the windows . . . I should be sitting in another room, rainbow-hued, looking not into the past but into the future: and I should not be sitting alone.

Most of us can quote the opening line of *The Go-Between*. Along with that of *Rebecca*, it is one that many an author must wish they had come up with themselves: 'The past is a foreign country: they do things differently there.'

During the dog days of July 1900, the 12-year-old Leo Colston goes to visit his schoolfriend Marcus Maudsley at his family's fine country house – though of course, in that foreign country of rigid prep-school protocol, they are plain 'Colston' and 'Maudsley' to one another. Leo, too young to comprehend the behaviour of grown-ups, becomes the unwitting conduit, the eponymous go-between, in what a tabloid newspaper today would no doubt brand a 'love triangle'.

But in 1900 there is no such language available to Leo to describe what he is so ill-equipped to understand. His actions are pivotal in the tragedy that unfolds, an experience of such emotional intensity that no one escapes unscathed, least of all the book's young narrator. As I said, an unusual book to give to an adolescent girl – and yet my mother adored north Norfolk; she spent the first ten years of her life near the coast here, until her father, a town planner, moved the family inland, close to where he was working on some of the hideous new conurbations around the M25. It was a wrench from which she never fully recovered.

She ensured that many of our childhood holidays were spent in Norfolk and once, walking in the grounds of Felbrigg Hall, taking a path around the lake, my mother told me that this was where the film of her favourite novel had been shot. We were taking the route that Leo ran along with notes from Marian, Marcus's older sister (played in the film by Julie Christie), to Ted Burgess (portrayed by Alan Bates), the tenant of Black Farm. I laboured under this misapprehension for many years, until a cursory Google search informed me that the house that stood in for Brandham was in fact Melton Constable Hall – a mere five miles from where we live now – while the village scenes were filmed at Heydon.

My mother was seduced, as the young Leo was, by the grandeur of Brandham Hall, the glamour of its occupants and the glorious golden Norfolk summer. When she was 19, a similar age to Marian, my mother, like her, became embroiled in an intoxicating affair with a man her parents considered beneath her. That relationship came to an abrupt and devastating end, too. In my mother's case, the recent passing into law of the Abortion Act of 1967 meant a different fate for her than that facing a hapless young woman in the summer of 1900.

'Our love was a beautiful thing, wasn't it?' says the elderly Marian to Leo in the book's closing pages, when he returns to Brandham to try to make sense of the catastrophe that has ruined his life.

> Do you remember what that summer was like? – how much more beautiful than any since? Well, what was the most beautiful thing in it? Wasn't it us, and our feelings for each other? Didn't you realize it, when you took our letters for us? Didn't you feel that all the rest – the house, the people coming and going – just didn't count?

'I did not understand the world of Brandham Hall,' the older Leo recalls; 'the people there were much larger than life.' The young Leo is acutely aware that he is of a lower social status. He lives quietly with his widowed mother in a modest house. Brandham Hall, with its cedar of Lebanon, its famous south-west prospect, its grand teas and revolving house guests, is another country again. And presiding over this whirlwind of gaiety is the formidable Mrs Maudsley and her wilful daughter Marian, reluctant to play the part she has been assigned. 'My sister is very beautiful,' Marcus informs

Leo. 'So that is what it is to be beautiful, I thought, and for a time, my idea of her as a person was confused and even eclipsed by the abstract idea of beauty that she represented.'

Leo is not of their world. His clothes are all wrong for the hot weather and it is Marian who, like 'a fairy princess', takes him shopping in Norwich, turning him 'from a laughing stock into an accepted member of her society'.

The Go-Between was published in 1953, the year before Nancy Mitford adopted the terms 'U' and 'non-U' for everday language, yet here is Marcus ticking off Leo in the summer of 1900: 'Marcus had told me that only an outsider spoke of a woman as a lady. It was one of his shibboleths.'

'Oughtn't I to call you my lord?' Leo asks of Trimingham, the hereditary owner of the Brandham estate (now let to Marcus's family) and to whom Marian is betrothed. It is a good match: the new money of the Maudsleys will enable the ninth Viscount to live in his own house once again, while Marian gains a title. Trimingham, perhaps the sole adult in the book whose behaviour is irreproachable, exhorts Leo to call him Hugh. 'I had taken a great liking to Lord Trimingham, though I couldn't have told whether I liked the Viscount or the man.' Much later, Leo will reproach himself: 'You flew too near the sun, and you were scorched.'

That far-flung country of 1900 is exquisitely evoked. Describing setting off for a bathing party, the older Leo explains that 'the word [bathing] denoted an intenser experience than it does now', and that while the bicycle Marian means to give him for his birthday might seem 'an anti-climax' to a child of today, 'to me it opened the gates of heaven'.

Twelve-year-olds were far more innocent then in other ways, too. 'The facts of life were a mystery to me,' says Leo. I don't think the word 'sex' appears in the book at all; 'spooning' is the term that Leo and Marcus use (with much hilarity), 'for it was the aspect of grown-up behaviour we found the silliest'. As Leo stumbles towards some sort of understanding of the true nature of the relationship between Marian and Ted which he has – unwittingly – facilitated by being their 'postman', he exclaims, in horror, 'I'm quite sure your sister Marian doesn't spoon . . . she's got too much sense.'

Matters of class, on the other hand, are always explicit, with transgressions taboo, unthinkable. 'We don't know him socially, of course,' says Marcus's older brother, Denys, on encountering Ted Burgess at the bathing spot. In contrast to Trimingham's cool demeanour, fine clothes and panama, Ted, Leo observes, is mature masculinity 'in its most undeniable form'. His skin is burnt the colour of 'a ripe cornfield in May', he is dangerous, animalistic, surrounded by the smell of horses, of manure, of the farmyard. 'It made me uncomfortable, almost giddy and yet it stimulated me,' says Leo.

Like all good books that we return to throughout our lives, *The Go-Between* yields something different on every reading. As a teenager longing for love, I ached for Marian and Ted and their impossible situation. Later, as the mother of young boys, I hated them for the way in which – to use another word alien to that foreign country – they groomed Leo to do their bidding. 'She was quick at finding out things', observes Leo of Marian, while Ted promises to tell him about 'spooning', but only if 'you carry on being our postman'.

This time, as I have read *The Go-Between* in the county in which it is set, I've noticed for the first time all sorts of things that L. P. Hartley must have observed. Trimingham is an actual place near Cromer. The multiple 'Burnham' villages surely inspired the 'Brandhams' in the book, and the county is full of those restricted byways which Leo notices as he rides beside the coachman on the carriage. I find that this time, with age and experience, I need to employ yet another word unknown in that distant country of 1900 to explain how I feel. For nothing in the story is binary. Marian is neither good nor bad; she is very young, she is trapped in a terrible predicament, as constrained by society as she is by her impractical clothes. 'Oh these dresses!' she exclaims, unable to conceal one of the notes Leo has brought her. Yes, Marian grooms Leo, but he is a willing participant, craving acceptance – 'how much diviner the air I now breathed . . . my old life was a discarded husk'. She uses Leo, she deceives him and yet she feels genuine affection for him. The passage in which Leo asks, 'But why are you going to marry Hugh if you don't want to?' is one of the very few from a grown-up book that has made me weep.

> 'Because I must marry him,' she said. 'You wouldn't understand. I *must*. I've *got* to!' Her lips trembled and she burst into tears . . . The sight of her tears loosened mine and I cried too. How long we cried I do not know.

Ted and Marian are wrong to carry on their affair once she is engaged to the decent, upstanding Trimingham. But is not the love between them pure and natural, 'a beautiful thing', the antithesis of her mother's house parties with 'people being paired off like animals at stud'? Their deceit ruins Leo's life, but in the 'sixty-odd' Leo, might we have an unreliable narrator, an embittered old man who has made bad choices (yet another foreign phrase) and whose disappointments cannot all be attributed to those nineteen days in July half a century earlier?

Perhaps that is what my mother bequeathed to me then; that life is vast and complicated and unfathomable. Happiness, when it presents itself, is so often fleeting, but we should grasp it, should live and love fiercely. The only curse, as the aged Marian tells Leo, in one of the last sentences she utters, is to live with 'an unloving heart'.

FLORA WATKINS lives in a farmhouse in north Norfolk with her family, a brace of basset hounds and six chickens named after the Mitford sisters.

Hooked on Fish

CHRISTIAN TYLER

Because they live on an island laced with rivers, ponds and streams, the British are obsessive anglers. Fishermen – and most of them are men – make up a large but secretive society cut off from the rest of us by strange language, obscure controversies and complex motives.

Most books about angling are written for specialists: coarse fishers, fly-fishers, sea-fishers. But in *Blood Knots* (2010) Luke Jennings has broken with convention and employed his great gift for words to explain to baffled outsiders what angling is really about. This is a memoir written for everyone.

The first few pages are a sublime description of a murky night fishing for pike on the Regent's Canal behind King's Cross railway station in London. It is a dark and dangerous place. You can almost hear the dripping walls and the rustle of rats and see, below the black oily surface of the water, tangles of twisted metal – and worse.

From an early age Jennings was dazzled by the beauty of fish: from the humble perch, the silvery roach, the brassy rudd, to the powerful carp and primitive pike with his wicked teeth, up to the aristocratic trout and salmon. He was obsessed by fishing tackle too: the strangely named floats and hooks, lines and lures, plugs, spinners, spoons and traces, swivels and booms, and the exotic flies – Tups, Duns, Olives, Adams, Humpy, John Storey and Cul de Canard.

I am no fisherman. But as a boy on holiday in Scotland, spinning for the monster pike rumoured to lurk in the 'bottomless' Loch Ussie or vainly flogging the River Conon for salmon, I learned enough to understand Jennings's passion and appreciate his philosophy. Much later in life I watched a fly-fisherman below Doune Castle unfurling his line in great aerial arabesques over the River Teith in Perthshire and felt pangs of admiration and envy.

A 'blood knot' is the commonest method of attaching one line to another. Here a fishing term stands also for the ties of family and friendship. For Jennings's book is not only a lyrical history of his angling life; it is also a wonderfully humorous account of his school-days and a tribute to the memory of two extraordinary heroes. One is his father Michael Jennings, a cavalry commander in the Second World War who was badly burned trying to rescue a comrade from their blazing tank and was awarded the Military Cross. The other is his fishing mentor, Robert Nairac, a soldier murdered by the IRA while working undercover for the SAS during the Troubles and awarded the George Cross.

Surviving his war, Michael Jennings became headmaster of Avisford, the Catholic preparatory school started by his own father in West Sussex. It was there as a 12-year-old pupil that Luke met Nairac, who had just left Ampleforth College (the 'Catholic Eton' which Michael and Luke Jennings both attended) and was putting in a year as a temporary teacher before going up to Oxford.

As it happens, I was also a pupil at both schools. My first sight of Michael Jennings's scarred face and permanently clenched hands was alarming; but we children soon got used to his injuries. He was a kind, intelligent man, generous and fatherly. Luke was born in 1953 during my first term at Avisford, the eldest of eleven children, and I think we were given a day off in celebration.

Avisford was a fine white mansion, once the home of G. A. Henty, the Victorian writer of derring-do historical fiction. It boasted a first-floor ballroom (which had become a dormitory) suspended from con-cealed chains, a big south-facing lawn, a bamboo 'jungle' and

fine specimen trees. Luke recalls how his
father allowed pupils to climb the trees
once they reached the age of 11, including
the fearsome 100-foot deodar from whose crow's nest of a crown –
once you found the courage to make the ascent – you could see for
miles, to Ford aerodrome and the sea.

Far below it were the cricket nets. It was there one day while we
were practising our leg sweeps that we were shocked by a big explosion. We looked up. Two aeroplanes had collided in mid-air and we
saw one of the pilots come floating down under his parachute. He
was later found dead, hanging from a tree in the wood across the
road. The more intrepid pupils went out illegally to hunt for sou-
venirs of the crash, scraps of metal which were vigorously traded.

Jennings is strangely reluctant to declare that Avisford was both
his home and his school. He describes the standard punishment for
serious rule-breaking: a single whack behind the thigh with the back
of a clothes-brush which left an impressive technicolour bruise.
Though the waiting, I recall, was much worse than the beating, he
omits to mention that it was his own father who administered it.
Perhaps this dissociation was due to respect for his father's memory.
Or perhaps he felt – as do all children sent to boarding-school – that
home and school are quite different worlds.

We first meet Robert Nairac when Jennings and two friends knock
on his door. He is lying on his bed in shirtsleeves, smoking. He has
just finished cleaning the 12-bore shotgun he has brought with him
to help feed the sparrowhawk he has lodged in the school shed.
Jennings immediately notices a large fishing bag on top of the chest
of drawers.

With this charismatic character as his guide, the boy's piscatorial
career is about to take off. In spite of his strong Catholic upbringing,
Jennings felt himself to be 'a believer searching for a belief'. The
Catholic Church seemed to him – as until very recently it was –
oblivious to God's creation, Nature. Now he had found a kindred

spirit, a mentor who 'preached the gospel of the dry fly'.

First there were casting lessons on the school lawn. At the end of the summer term Nairac invited Jennings to his home in the Cotswolds for some grown-up fishing. And when that autumn his pupil went up to Ampleforth, the former head boy and champion angler twice drove from Oxford to Yorkshire to check on his progress.

The author is in lighter vein when he describes his formal education. As he says, some teachers are inspiring, some eccentric, some are both. The tedious ones could be flattered into retailing their wartime exploits. One of my classics masters had been at the Siege of Kut in the First World War. Asked if he'd been forced to eat rats, he protested not: he'd survived by reading the lyric verse of *The Greek Anthology*.

There was a brilliant maths teacher at Avisford, Mr Vinycombe, who made differential calculus look as easy as π. At Ampleforth we both encountered M. Cossart, a little old French grammarian who had taught Jennings's father in the 1930s; he rewarded his prize pupils with a cream tea in the village. Both of us had teachers – one a historian, the other a classicist – who would break, unprovoked, into long declamations from the tragedies of Corneille or Racine. And we both profited from the inspiring drama of Algy Haughton's lessons in English literature.

Of course there were other masters who indulged in what Jennings deftly describes as 'lower-slopes paedophilia', like the music master at Avisford who composed four-part settings of the Mass for us to sing and was rumoured to have kissed a boy. There was also a popular gym teacher who sold us balsa-wood aircraft kits and taught us to swing Indian clubs, but before each lesson he would line us up and squeeze our thighs. One boy told his father, a senior army officer, who drove down and had the man sacked on the spot. Serious offenders were rare but Ampleforth's own prep school, Gilling Castle, had a priest who was later jailed for indecent assault.

After school Luke Jennings trained as a dancer at the Rambert School, became dance critic of the *Observer*, worked as a freelance journalist and novelist. His *Codename Villanelle* trilogy about a female professional assassin pursued by a female secret agent was the basis of the hit BBC television series *Killing Eve*. But he never stopped fishing. From throwing bread or worms to pond fish in Sussex, he moved to fly-fishing for trout on the chalk streams of Hampshire and Wiltshire. His youthful urge to kill, show off, then eat his catch was displaced by an almost reverential concern for it: after taking a moment to judge its weight and admire its looks, he would return his fish to the water.

The sporting angler is like the sporting gun who prefers to go after woodcock or snipe because they are wild, elusive and beautiful, rather than mass-reared pheasant or partridge. But the shooter, of course, kills his prey. Like a game shooter, Jennings remembers every moment of his best hits and worst misses. He relishes that contrast between the long, meditative hours of waiting and the suspense and sudden excitement, even panic, of the moment when he must strike.

The true angler, he says, can feel the antiquity of the countryside through which he moves. It is a form of time travel, 'a return of the dewy, spring morning of his life, when anything is possible'. And his observance of self-imposed rules of conduct, as explained by Robert Nairac, is a sacred duty. 'It's not a question of wilfully making things harder, but of a purity of approach without which success has no meaning . . . the fiercest joy is to be a spectator of your own conduct and find no cause for complaint.'

So if you win the battle of wits with your fish, you must be humble and put him back. For his life is totally entwined, like a blood knot, with yours.

CHRISTIAN TYLER is writing a book about the first clash of cultures between Europe and China and thinks that we could all take a leaf out of this one.

The vignettes that appear in this article and which illustrate our edition of *Blood Knots* are by Caroline Churchill.

Luke Jennings's *Blood Knots* (224pp) is now available in a limited and numbered cloth-bound edition of 2,000 copies (subscribers: UK & Eire £18, Overseas £20; non-subscribers: UK & Eire £20, Overseas £22). All prices include post and packing. Copies may be ordered by post (53 Hoxton Square, London N1 6PB), by phone (020 7033 0258) or via our website www.foxedquarterly.com.

See also Tortoise

LAURA FREEMAN

'It's like Pokémon,' said my husband Andy, standing in the cool of a church in San Gimignano on our very hot honeymoon. And yes, I suppose saint-spotting is a bit like Pokémon, the creature-collecting game invented by Nintendo in the Nineties. Slogan: 'Gotta catch 'em all.'

We weren't hunting for Pikachus or Bulbasaurs, but for St Catherines and St Antony Abbots in fresco cycles and altarpiece panels. Catherine you'll know by her wheel, instrument of her martyrdom, St Antony by his bell and his pig. A friend speaks fondly of childhood holidays with his church-crawling parents. He and his twin sister would be sent off to play saintly bingo. Could they find a St John the Baptist (lamb and sheepskin gilet), a Mary Magdalene (jar of unguent), an Apollonia (tooth and pincers)? Off they would go round cloisters, into side-chapels, standing on tiptoe for a better look at stained-glass windows. As with Pokémon, they knew their saints by their markers. Gotta catch 'em all.

I came to the game later. It would be nice to tell you of a Road to Damascus moment (see PAUL, the conversion of), of picking up a copy of *Hall's Dictionary of Subjects and Symbols in Art* from a shelf in a second-hand bookshop and being blinded by the light of sudden art-historical revelation. In truth, *Hall's* was a set book on a university reading list. I ordered a copy and put it in a box in the boot of a car bound for Freshers' Week. No one sits down to read a dictionary. I'd look at it as and when.

James Hall, *Hall's Dictionary of Subjects and Symbols in Art* (1974)
Revised edition (2014) · Routledge · Pb · 41opp · £39.99 · ISBN 9780813343938

But *Hall's* isn't a dictionary, alphabetically arranged though it is. I was going to say that it's more of a gazetteer, a guide to people, paintings and putti. But gazetteer isn't quite right either. Too workaday. *Hall's* is more like a grimoire – a magician's manual for invoking strange beings and things. Hammer, Hand, Hare, Harp, Harpy, Harrowing of Hell, Harvest, Hat, Hatchet . . . Such summonings can be glorious – a Harp appears commonly among the instruments played by concerts of angels – and they can be gory. One may find a Hatchet 'embedded in the skull of Dominican monk, the attribute of PETER MARTYR.'

Hall's sets the hares running. It's not just for Christmas presents and it's certainly not just for reference. It's a dictionary you really do read. When I can't sleep, I open it at random and see where the pages fall. Peace, Peach, Peacock, Pearl, Pegasus, Pelias (king of Iolcus, see JASON; MEDEA), Pelican, '*Pellit et attrahit*' (see WINDS), Pelt, Pen and inkhorn (see WRITER) . . . And if you think I chose that page deliberately, so that I'd land on pen and inkhorn and a point about writing, I didn't. Serendipity. With Hall, there's a Peach on every page. It's not a book you need read in order, working your way down the list. Better to let yourself be blown off course. Interest piqued by '*Pellit et attrahit*'? Here it is under Winds: 'A bodiless wind god is the *impresa* of Ranuccio Farnese, Duke of Parma (1569–1622), with the motto "*Pellit et attrahit*" – "He drives off (evil) and attracts (good)". (Farnese Palace, Rome.) See also SAIL.'

Sail. The attribute of FORTUNE, both in antiquity and the Renaissance, because she is inconstant like the wind; also of VENUS, who was born of the sea. A sail-like drapery billowing over the head of a sea-nymph, see GALATEA. See also TORTOISE.

Tortoise, with a sail on its back, was the *impresa* of Cosimo de' Medici (1369–1464). The accompanying motto was '*Festina lente*' – 'Make haste slowly', that is be slow but sure.

Slow but sure was the James Hall way. He worked steadily, tire-lessly at his *Dictionary* over many years. His research was rewarded. Published in 1974, *Hall's Dictionary of Subjects and Symbols in Art* is still in print and has been translated into twelve languages. My paperback edition is introduced by Kenneth Clark, otherwise Lord Clark of *Civilisation*. He begins by informing us that fifty years ago (the 1920s) we were told that 'subject' no longer mattered in art. It was all about form, or 'significant form' as it was then fashionably called.

This was a curious aberration of criticism, because all artists from the cave painters onwards, had attached great importance to their subject matter; Giotto, Giovanni Bellini, Titian, Michelangelo, Poussin or Rembrandt would have thought it incredible that so absurd a doctrine could have gained currency.

Worse, in that same fifty years,

the average man had become progressively less able to recognize the subjects or understand the meaning of the works of art of the past. Fewer people had read the classics of Greek and Roman literature, and relatively few people read the Bible with the same diligence that their parents had done. It comes as a shock to an elderly man to find how many biblical references have become completely incomprehensible to the present generation.

Clark would be more shocked still at the incomprehension of my generation of millennials when presented with a painting of, say, The Visitation (the pregnant Virgin Mary and her cousin Elizabeth meet-ing bump-to-bump). 'What the ordinary traveller with an interest in art and a modicum of curiosity requires is a book which will tell him the meaning of subjects which every amateur would have recognized from the middle ages down to the late eighteenth century.' Such a book is *Hall's*.

James Hall was an ordinary sort of traveller with an extraordinary turn of mind. He was born on 8 July 1918, in Norton, near Baldock, Hertfordshire, where his father owned a farm. He had little formal education, left school at 17, and went into commercial advertising. When the war came, he successfully claimed exemption from military service as a conscientious objector. In 1940, he volunteered for the Friends' Ambulance Service and served with a military mobile hospital in North Africa and then Syria. After the war, he worked for the publishers J. M. Dent, later becoming production manager at the Dent head office in Bedford Street, Covent Garden, where he supervised the publication of the Everyman's Library. Motto: 'I will go with thee, and be thy guide/ In thy most need go by thy side.'

In his spare time Hall taught himself French, Italian and Spanish with the help of language-learning vinyl records. When lunch hours allowed, he would visit the National Gallery and find himself puzzling over saints and their attributes. Hall looked for a book that would explain why that lady was bearing her breasts on a plate (poor, poor St Agatha) and what that chap was doing writing books in the desert (St Jerome, with lion and pen). Finding no such volume, he set out, Jerome-like, to write it himself. He didn't stick to saints. In *Hall's* you'll find gods and monsters, heroes and hedgehogs, Polyphemus the one-eyed cyclops and Pasiphae 'who conceived a violent and unnatural passion for a bull'.

Hall would get up at 6 a.m. to work for an hour at home in Harpenden before taking a train into London. After a day at Dent, he would pick up again in the evenings. Weekends he spent in the Reading Room at the British Museum, in the National Art Library at the Victoria and Albert Museum or at the London Library. Remember, this was in the days before search engines or digital library catalogues. It took Hall years to produce what he modestly called *The Dictionary of Subjects and Symbols in Art*. His publisher, John Murray, rightly rechristened it *Hall's Dictionary*. Kenneth Clark wrote that he would recommend *Hall's* 'to anyone who wishes to increase his interest and pleasure in visiting a picture gallery or turning over the illustrations of a book on art'. Reading *Hall's* is a pleasure in itself, but Clark is correct: far better is the pleasure it brings to looking at pictures.

In the Discworld books *Thud!* and *Making Money*, Terry Pratchett has his characters visit the collection of the Ankh Morpork city art gallery which contains such masterpieces as Carvatti's *Three Large Pink Women and One Piece of Gauze*, Sir Robert Cuspidor's *Wagon Stuck in River*, Mauvaise's sculpture *Man with Big Figleaf* and an unrivalled collection of pictures of women with not many clothes on, posing by an urn.

When looking at pictures, there is, of course, no need to know the narrative. You could simply admire the brushstrokes, the *chiaroscuro*, the *contrapposto*, the *sfumato*, the fine handling of paint in *Man and Woman Naked with Tree Snake*, *Large Pink Woman with Bull by the Sea* or the famous *Haircut by Candlelight*. But you might get rather more out of the 'Temptation', the 'Rape of Europa' and 'Samson and Delilah' if you knew who's who and what's what. Perhaps what it boils down is this: I like stories. I like them a great deal more than I like form, significant or otherwise. *Hall's* is full of them. From the Old and New Testaments, from the *Iliad* and the *Odyssey*, from Ariosto and Ovid. Stories apocryphal, stories mythological, stories miraculous and stories diabolical. Stories about a man and his three-headed dog. *Hall's* has it all.

When Andy and I were struggling for baby names last year, I found myself flicking through *Hall's*. Aeneas? Angelica? Demeter? Dorothea? Elmo? Euphemia? Iphigenia? (Effie? Iffie?). 'Alice is nice,' Andy would counter. Or Anne. Or Josh. Or Rob. Or any other name less tragic, Greek or polysyllabic. As the due date drew nearer, we both warmed to Arthur, if a boy, while I petitioned for Iris, my grandmother's name, if a girl. I consulted *Hall's* to check that Iris was not an ancient goddess of strife. Happily, not.

Iris in Greek mythology was the goddess who personified the rainbow, on which she descended to earth as messenger of the gods. Juno sent Iris to release the soul of Dido when she died on the pyre. She was sent to rouse the sleeping Morpheus (SLEEP, KINGDOM OF).

Andy fancied Nancy, but on the day, when the baby appeared, she was definitely not an Arthur, and not quite a Nancy either. The I's had it. She was Iris Irena after my grandma and Andy's Polish grandmother. ('Irene – according to legend, a widow of Rome who cared for ST SEBASTIAN and nursed him back to health after he had been left for dead, his body full of arrows. She is hence a patron saint of nurses.') Opening *Hall's* where it falls in the small hours with a very small Iris asleep across my lap, I alight on the L's: Lily, Limbo, Lion, Lizard, Loaves and Fishes, multiplication of, Loincloth, Longinus, Loom . . . Is that not strange and evocative? Does that not conjure a gallery of paintings familiar, once seen and long forgotten? With *Hall's* you never know where the winds – see Aeolus, see Boreas, see Flora, see Zephyr – may take you.

LAURA FREEMAN (see Laurel, Apollo, Daphne, Parnassus and Aspergillum) is chief art critic for *The Times* and author of *Ways of Life: Jim Ede and the Kettle's Yard Artists* (2023). You can hear her in Episode 30 of our podcast, 'Jim Ede's Way of Life', talking about art in the 1920s.

In Love with the League

ROBIN BLAKE

I once had what I thought was a pretty good idea for a spy novel set in the 1920s. The hero would be a shell-shocked war veteran who winds up in a clinic in Switzerland being psychoanalysed by someone vaguely like Carl Jung. A fellow patient is an attractive woman working for the brand-new League of Nations in Geneva and, as they start an affair, he discovers she – and the League – possess a secret on which the future of world peace hinges . . . I was vague on the details.

It felt less like a good idea after I'd outlined it to a friend. He looked incredulous. 'You want to set a thriller in the League of Nations? Where's the excitement in that?'

The League grew out of the trauma of Passchendaele, Verdun and Gallipoli at the urging of the US president, Woodrow Wilson, with the objective of calming everybody down and making all future wars unnecessary. Wilson, however, couldn't persuade his own Congress to let America join, leaving the League largely to a handful of more-or-less two-faced British and French statesmen.

It settled into what had been a grand hotel, the Palais Wilson, in harmless, neutral Geneva, where representatives of forty-two nations enjoyed a beautiful lake view as they wrestled with the status of questionable territories (the Saar, Danzig), border disputes (Albania, Colombia/Peru) and former German and Turkish colonies (Palestine, Lebanon, South-West Africa). But, although small triumphs were achieved, the grand plan to superannuate international warfare was a

---

Frank Moorhouse's *Grand Days* (1993) and *Dark Palace* (2000) are out of print, but we can obtain second-hand copies.

Emery Kelen (1896–1978) was a sort of in-house cartoonist for the League of Nations and drew hundreds of caricatures of League people, including this one, drawn in 1925 to celebrate a press lunch

disastrous flop. All too often the League looked like a dog chasing its own tail.

Where, indeed, is the excitement in that?

But sometimes a dull dog has a fascinating inner life, and it took the enterprise and talent of the Australian novelist Frank Moorhouse to illuminate the Jungian shadow of the League of Nations. His *Grand Days* (1993) and *Dark Palace* (2000) form an epic diptych of over a thousand pages, set entirely in the League between the mid-

1920s and 1945. It is not (or not primarily) a spy story but a doomed romance. A young Australian girl, Edith Campbell Berry, comes to Geneva and falls in love with her employer. The love object however is not a person, it is an institution: Edith falls head over heels for the League of Nations itself and, as the two novels progress, we follow that love's course through delight, disappointment, furious rows, betrayal, reconciliation and, at the end, tearful annihilation.

It all begins in a sunburst of hope. Taking up her post at the start of *Grand Days*, Edith fully expects to change the world, while opening herself to all the experiences of a modern self-actuating woman. 'She believed that she and the others at the League were a new breed dawning. She did not think that being in her mid-twenties was too late to refashion oneself, while still keeping a grip of political realism.' That last proviso turns out to be one of the novels' keys. Although there is plenty of humour, both broad and subtle, in these books, Moorhouse avoids the easy path of lampooning the League of Nations as a futile talking-shop, as many contemporaries did.

> Like leaves in Vallombrosa,
> Tobacco in Virginia,
> Like monks on Monte Rosa,
> And chiefs in Abyssinia,
> Like banditry in China,
> Or Turkomen in Khiva,
> Like herring in Loch Fyne are
> Committees in Geneva.

The satirist's point would be quite lost on Edith Campbell Berry. She revels in committees as

> parlour games where each person's contribution was their throw of the dice, from which followed certain moves around the board. For her, committees were the Great Basic Unit. When you understood the workings of a committee . . . you under-

stood the workings of an empire. Of course there should be a place in administration for dashing individualism and grand leadership but in her experience it was never a bad thing for lofty plans to be brushed down and combed by the committee.

The world's addiction to war is not the only item on the League's agenda. There are also knotty social issues, most of them still with us – the rights of women and refugees, racism, modern slavery, drug trafficking, decolonization, world health. Edith often finds these matters reflecting back on herself and her personal relationships. So, just as the League grapples with questions around overpopulation and eugenics, Edith must consider the implications of her use of a contraceptive device that she gets by mail order from Germany.

The moral equivalence of public policy and personal life is a recurrent theme. In one episode Captain Strongbow, an American charlatan, persuades Edith to parade through the Geneva streets dressed as a cowgirl, as an advertisement for his idea of a 'world police force'. She surprises herself by getting a strong kick out of this extrovert display but she also discovers that 'good ideas were sometimes propounded by people who were not always personally sound and not always decorous'.

Another insight comes to her in a jazz club where a black musician, Jerome, explains the wordless singing called scat: 'scat is the sound you speak when you are not speaking'. Tipsy on champagne she makes a series of connections 'where sound became music; where music became jazz; where jazz became poetry; where poetry became scat singing; where scat singing became meaning' and suddenly she is thinking about international communication across language barriers. 'My God! It's a new parlance!' Later in the evening, alone with Jerome, Edith uses her own mouth in a way that is also other than speaking, and an equally 'new parlance'. So the path of Edith's sexual education is tracked in parallel with her growth as a diplomat.

As she develops and changes Edith sees how relations, whether international or interpersonal, depend on 'civilized tenets', that is on comity, and on protocol which is 'formalized goodwill'. Treaties are really only the same as handshakes, deals based on trust. But 'when the trust has gone so has civilization'. She also learns about the worm that eats into and destroys this trust: the principle of *rebus sic stantibus* ('things thus standing') by which a treaty can be broken when its background conditions may have shifted. Hitler invades the Rhineland on this pretext. Edith finds the same tactic being used – by herself and others – in her own private liaisons.

The most significant of these is with an older Englishman at the League, the suave and worldly-wise Ambrose Westwood. They meet and flirt on the train on their way to Geneva and later embark on an affair that will be the most important of Edith's life. It is also the most unusual, since Ambrose turns out to enjoy putting on Edith's clothes and soon leads her into an unsuspected network of cross-dressing and gender fluidity alongside, and sometimes overlapping, that of the dull dogs of the League.

A man writing about the perceptions and feelings of a strong female protagonist needs to be, in a literary sense, a cross-dresser himself. Some culture warriors would use the term 'cultural appropriation' for male novelists who do this, which would seem to judge Flaubert, Thackeray or James Joyce rather harshly. To me Frank Moorhouse's heroine is as fully realized as Madame Bovary, Becky Sharp or Molly Bloom.

Edith is a devoted self-observer, constantly cross-checking her intimate thoughts and reflections as they change and contradict each other. In the beginning she has a private range of social responses, ready for use in any given circumstance, which she calls her Ways: the Way of Companionable Directness, the Way of the Silent Void or, when the situation gets out of hand, the Way of Cowardly Flight. But she draws less and less on these Ways as she gains confidence, and then something of Flora Poste in *Cold Comfort Farm* develops in Edith. She is an organizer, increasingly driven not by instinct but by an enquiring rationalism. She is open to new experience, whether sensual or intellectual, but is increasingly possessed of a beady eye for humbug and bad faith. Another protagonist she reminds me of is Harriet Pringle in Olivia Manning's Balkan and Levant trilogies (see *SF* nos. 63 and 64). Frequently buffeted by world events and troublesome personal relationships, both women guard their integrity and dignity as best they can – and do not always succeed.

While *Grand Days* plays out in the jazzy 1920s, *Dark Palace* deals with the League's second, gloomier decade. Edith and her colleagues now face a string of international crises – Abyssinia, Spain, the aggression of Nazi Germany. The outbreak of the Second World War leaves the still new Palais des Nations (which has replaced the Palais Wilson) stripped down to a skeleton staff who go on issuing reports and statistics for a world that is no longer listening. There is real pathos in this.

> Edith stopped at the Council Room and looked in at the green covers fitted to the round dais and benches, where once five hundred delegates had gathered. She glanced at the murals, 'The End of Pestilence', 'Strength', 'Law', 'The End of Slavery', 'Solidarity of Peoples', 'The End of War'. All closed now. All unseen and unbelieved. The murals spoke only to themselves.

After the war, a conference is called in San Francisco to institute a new world body and Edith and her remaining colleagues stand ready to be integrated into what they expect to be the 'New League of Nations', this time boosted by the United States as a member. To their shock and pain it doesn't work out like that and they and the League are cruelly consigned to the dark and ignominious dustbin of history. When the despairing Edith asks Ambrose, 'Did we waste our lives at the League? All those words we wrote and spoke?' he can only answer, 'There is no one to tell us whether we did, or did not.'

ROBIN BLAKE's latest novel *Hungry Death* came out in 2022.

A Damn Good Chap

LAURIE GRAHAM

Gone are the days when children could be out of the house from breakfast till suppertime, messing about in boats or dangling over cliffs searching for birds' eggs, and no one would give them a second thought. Hilary Hook, born in 1917, grew up in Devon in one such benignly neglectful family. In his late sixties he became, to his surprise, a household name, following the screening of Molly Dineen's 1984 documentary *Home from the Hill*.

This was the story of Hilary, the old colonial hand, aware of encroaching age in a changing world, who returned to England and exchanged life in an idyllic, if quirkily staffed Kenyan bungalow, bursting at the seams with what he referred to as 'personal gubbins', for a small, unstaffed house in Wiltshire. I had remembered that documentary, not least for the moment when the former Great White Hunter was defeated by a can-opener and a tin of ravioli. 'Damn it,' he said, 'I'll go to the pub.' So I was delighted to discover that Hilary Hook had written a memoir, its title, like that of the film which preceded it, borrowed from lines by Robert Louis Stevenson:

> Here he lies where he longed to be;
> Home is the sailor, home from sea,
> And the hunter home from the hill.

Prep school appears to have made little impact on Hilary's ragamuffin childhood spent sailing, rabbiting, and hunting on a borrowed

---

Hilary Hook's *Home from the Hill* (1987) is out of print, but we can obtain second-hand copies.

cob, except, perhaps, for the influence of a kindly headmaster who had been in the Indian Army, and the school's annual visit to the home of a retired big game hunter. Young Hilary began to dream of India and Africa.

His mother, a genteel widow, thought he'd better go to Oxford and then into the Colonial Service. Hilary saw himself as a game warden in East Africa. The matter was resolved one winter evening

when Mrs Hook read aloud to him from a new book sent to her by the subscription library: *The Lives of a Bengal Lancer* by F. Yeats-Brown. For Hilary there was no longer any doubt. He'd cram for the Sandhurst entrance exams, face the rigours of officer training and join the Indian Army. By the age of 20 he was on his way, shipping out to Allahabad via Karachi. His task, to learn some Urdu and find a place for himself in an Indian regiment. He also learned to play polo and shoot crocodile.

It was 1938 and there was a growing threat of war, but the Royal Deccan Horse was still a mounted regiment. *Home from the Hill* (1987) describes cavalry training in the hills of Baluchistan, with iced beer and luncheon delivered by regimental camel. There were encounters with Afghan caravans heading south, laden with carpets and spices, and there was jackal-hunting with the Peshawar Vale foxhounds.

Molly Dineen

Hilary had a short war. Though his regiment dismounted and learned to drive tanks, their deployment was constantly delayed. In frustration he asked to be sent to Burma to fight with the Chindits and spent Christmas Day 1943 in Port Moresby, New Guinea, playing cricket against eleven ageing Australian quartermasters and storemen. The British, he tells us, won by one run.

Back in post-war, pre-partition India we begin to see a change in Hilary. Formerly an enthusiastic hunter of game, big and small, he describes the high tension of a shoot, tracking and pursuing a tiger known to be killing livestock, and then his remorse at the sight of the magnificent animal he has felled with a single shot. In future, he vows, he will shoot only for food or, if pushed, to kill a tiger that has been identified as a man-eater. His childhood dream of being a game warden has resurfaced. He is advised, though, that it is a job that pays peanuts, suitable only for a man of private means, and Hilary has none. Instead he signs on for a stint with the Sudan Defence Force.

Several times during my reading of this short memoir I needed to get out my atlas: to follow, for instance, his voyage by wood-fuelled paddle-steamer, up the Nile to Equatorial Sudan. This was a man's world: long, arduous hikes and manoeuvres, shooting birds for the pot, and drinking sundowners with damned good chaps. The rare females who crop up are the kind who are willing to do the drudgery, shopping in Khartoum for groceries and kitchen equipment. Splendid gals. 'What on earth is a colander?' wonders Company Commander Hook, scanning a list of recommended camping supplies.

Then, more than halfway through the book, something extraordinary happens. Hilary gets married. He is 34 and army life has enabled him to put a bit by, so nothing notable there. What is astonishing is that the marriage is dealt with in a single paragraph. We are told the name of the Kenyan village where it took place, we know the name of the commanding officer he approached for approval of wedding-leave, but of the wife, nothing. She only reappears, shadow-like in the 1960s, as an ex-wife. Also, presumably, as the mother of his two sons.

Marriage apparently made little impact on Hilary's life. He took his bride to his new posting in Northern Sudan. When on duty, he led camel patrols; off-duty he learned Arabic and played polo. We read of a close encounter with a 12-foot python, but of Mrs Hook not a whisper. Was it a matter of valorous discretion or of self-absorbed cluelessness? Though his blokeish charm was very evident in Molly Dineen's film, my money is on the latter.

Hilary's life crisscrossed the world with occasional furloughs in England or, preferably, in Scotland or Ireland for good fly-fishing. From Sudan to Hong Kong, then to Aden and eventually back to Sudan to the boring desk duties of a military attaché. 'Too many parties,' he remembers, 'with too little whisky and too much warm soda water.'

In his late forties Hilary quit the army. He'd been offered a job as a game warden at the famous Treetops Hotel in Aberdare National Park, Kenya. His deferred dream was about to come true and in due course he and a friend set up a safari company. The only kind of shooting to be done was with cameras. They ranged across the borders of Kenya, Tanzania and Uganda, living under canvas and showing guests the birdlife and butterflies as well as the Big Five: elephant, lion, buffalo, leopard and rhino. In the wet seasons, April and November, he would retire to the veranda of his house in Kiserian which, like Isak Dinesen's African farm, was 'at the foot of the Ngong hills'.

By the early 1980s the safari scene was changing. The Tanzanian and Ugandan border areas were either dangerous or inaccessible and the Kenyan reserves were becoming victims of their own popularity, overrun with zebra-striped minibuses and tourists seeking a 24-hour safari experience. At the annual Shikar Club beano at the Savoy in London, Hilary Hook's death was announced prematurely. He was in fact alive and well and sleeping off a good dinner at the Muthaiga Club in Nairobi. But his Kenya days were numbered. His rented house was sold and its new owner demanded vacant possession. At the age of 67 Hilary decided to call it quits and return to England. Home was the hunter.

I learned many things from his book, some more useful than others. That in the Sudan, back in the day, elephant ivory was effectively a currency, useful for paying the grocer, often a Greek or an Armenian. That a squashed watermelon is an effective way to cool an overheated carburettor should that misfortune befall you far from roadside assistance. And that, though not recommended, it is possible to mount and ride an ostrich.

I'm conscious that there was a personal element to my enjoyment of Hilary's memoir. He evokes, for instance, a taste of one of the most challenging and hostile landscapes: the North-West Frontier. It was a place where, two generations earlier, my grandfather fought in the Malakand Rising. But I sense there is a more universal appeal. Hilary writes of a way of life that has completely disappeared. In his heyday there still existed areas of uncharted territory, with the very real possibility of being cut off from rescue or support. It is something hard for us to imagine in these days of super-connectivity. Self-reliance, and a willingness to make decisions and take responsibility for others, were paramount. In short, he makes our well-appointed and safety-conscious lives seem dull. These days even an East African safari is conducted in upholstered comfort.

Hilary Hook died in 1990, having enjoyed a late career as an entertaining relic of Empire. He was 72 but looked older, kippered by cigarettes and sun. 'Long years in bad stations,' he explained. In his Wiltshire retirement he apparently learned how to use a remote control to navigate Ceefax and check the cricket scores, but I suspect he never did fathom the purpose of a colander.

LAURIE GRAHAM is a retired novelist and journalist who, like Hilary Hook, never really put down roots. She laments the fact that genuine adventure has been safety-packaged out of existence. Now, without recourse to surgery or hormones, she is a Brother of the London Charterhouse.

The Littlest Ship

ANDREW JOYNES

It was a sparkling, blowsy, kiss-me-quick day beside the seaside. The flotilla of Little Ships was coming back to Ramsgate from its anniversary visit to Dunkirk. There was an air of excitement among the crowds lining the harbour wall as the first of the veteran boats was spotted far out on the sunlit water.

A woman in eighteenth-century costume stood beside the lighthouse. She reminded me of Gillray's cartoon of Emma Hamilton: of generous proportions, wearing a flimsy muslin dress with red, white and blue ribbons sewn into the hem, and sporting a wide bonnet with the same patriotic colours across the turned-up brim. As each of the boats came through the harbour entrance, she braced herself like an athlete preparing to throw the hammer, and then swung an enormous football rattle round in front of her. Delighted by the staccato noise, the crews in the Little Ships laughed and waved.

British Legion veterans solemnly lowered banners to salute the return of each boat. Like the lady in the patriotic dress, these elderly men with their berets and white gauntlets had been standing by the lighthouse for hours. As one of the Dunkirk vessels – a fire-fighting barge from the Thames docks – loosed off its hoses in a multiple spray that arced high into the air, the sergeant in charge of the Legion squad shouted, 'Don't look at it, boys! It'll make you want to go!'

The crowds cheered, the sun shone, the Sea Cadet band played,

Paul Gallico's *The Snow Goose* (1941) is available in a paperback edition, combined with *The Small Miracle*, from Penguin: 80pp · £7.99 · ISBN 9780140299526.

and flags waved. This was what celebration of Operation Dynamo – the so-called 'Miracle of Dunkirk' – meant decades after the event. On that anniversary day, I sensed the light-hearted striking of a defiant pose against a historical backdrop which, like a harbour wall, is lapped by tides of popular memory.

When Paul Gallico's story *The Snow Goose* was first published in the American *Saturday Evening Post* in the autumn of 1940, there was nothing about Britain's circumstances to lighten the hearts of Americans like himself who had travelled in Europe, seen Nazism at close hand and learned to detest it. America had not yet joined the war and, in the summer a few months before, over 300,000 British and Allied troops had been rescued from the beaches and shallows of Dunkirk, with trawlers, motor-boats, yachts and launches – the so-called 'Little Ships' – playing a key part in the rescue. Most of the exhausted soldiers were taken to ports like Ramsgate and disembarked along the harbour walls. *Perfugium Miseris* is the motto carved into the granite of the lighthouse at the harbour entrance: 'Safety for the Storm-tossed'.

Gallico made his name as a sports reporter for the *New York Daily News* in the 1920s, and once wrote about being knocked out by the heavyweight boxing champion Jack Dempsey. Fearless in search of a story, he had offered himself as a sparring partner and, confident that his New York readership would understand the literary references, he compared Dempsey to David, Siegfried and Roland.

But Gallico always wanted to write fiction, what he later called 'great' stories. In 1936, disillusioned at what he saw as the end of a heroic age of American sport, he moved to England and then travelled through Europe. His father was an Italian composer, and his mother was Austrian, and he felt his family background represented the cultural dignity of Europe that was threatened by fascism. Fiction might be a means of reasserting that dignity. 'It is a fact,' he wrote, 'startling perhaps in its implications, that fiction has far greater propaganda value, and gains far more credence among readers, than actuality.'

He realized that a story linked to the Dunkirk evacuation – however tenuously – was the 'great' story he had been searching for. 'Nothing that has happened in the war has captured my imagination as much as the evacuation of Dunkirk.'

And so he wrote *The Snow Goose*. It was described as a novella, but it is in fact a short story which takes no more than half an hour to read. The Dunkirk scenes, which come at the end, take up only a few pages. The setting for most of the story is what Gallico called 'one of the last of the wild places of England', a stretch of marshland on the Essex coast at the mouth of the Thames estuary where it opens to meet the wide horizons of the North Sea.

Following his move from New York Gallico travelled through England and became fascinated by the historical layers of the various English regions, particularly those along the east coast where invading Germanic tribes – Angles, Saxons, Jutes – settled after the Romans left. In *The Snow Goose* Gallico delights in the ancient customs of the Essex coast, relishing Saxon names like that of the hamlet of Wickaeldroth, and Frith, the name of the young girl who is one of the three central characters of his story.

The other human character is Philip Rhyader, a wildlife artist and recluse who lives in a deserted lighthouse far out on the Great Marsh. He is disabled, with a twisted spine and a malformed arm, and he both shuns and is shunned by the few people who find their way on to the mudflats – wildfowlers, mostly, who resent his attempts to protect the flocks of over-wintering birds that settle around his home.

The third central presence in the story is one of those wild birds – the Snow Goose, a rare incomer from Canada. It is a beautiful creature – purest white with black wing-tips – which has been blown off course by an Arctic storm, whirled across the Atlantic and then wounded by a hunter's gun on the edge of the marsh. Barely alive, it is found by the young girl Frith, who brings it to Rhyader in the hope that it will be healed by this malformed man who, despite his frightening appearance, always shows kindness to wild creatures.

The bird is indeed healed and becomes the
pretext for Frith to make return visits to the lighthouse. This distinctive creature, its plumage gleaming
like ice among the drab colours of the marshland, is the focus
of a child's wonder. Over the years, as the child becomes a woman,
as the Snow Goose departs each spring on migration with the pink-
footed geese with which it now associates – and then faithfully
returns in the autumn – it becomes a symbol of the growing relationship between Rhyader and Frith. Then one year it does not depart on
migration but stays. 'This is her home now,' says Rhyader, 'of her
own free will.'

At this point the rhythm of the story changes, becoming urgent
and impressionistic. One day Frith comes to the lighthouse and finds
Rhyader stowing provisions in his sailing dinghy: he is going to sail
to Dunkirk to help with the evacuation. 'Men are huddled on the
beaches like hunted birds, Frith, like the wounded and hunted birds
we used to find and bring to sanctuary . . .' As he sets off on his
journey, the Snow Goose follows, flying above him in slow, wide
circles. 'White sail and white bird were visible for a long time . . .'

Now the story takes on the quality of myth. The reader learns
about Rhyader's exploits at Dunkirk – and about the Snow Goose
hovering above him as he hauls men into the dinghy to carry them
from the beaches to the waiting Royal Navy ships – by overhearing a
conversation in a pub, where a couple of Cockney soldiers are swap-
ping stories.

'A goose, a bloomin' goose, so 'elp me. It come flyin' down out
of the muck an' stink an' smoke of Dunkirk. It was white, wiv
black on its wings, an' it circles us like a bloomin' dive bomber.
And then around a bend 'e comes in a bloody little sailboat,
sailing along as cool as you please . . .'

And so the reader eavesdrops as the soldiers drink their watery
wartime beer and tell how Rhyader ferried six or seven of them at a

time out to the waiting ships, his good hand on the tiller and the rope of the main sheets clasped between his teeth. 'An' over'ead all the time, around and around, flies the ruddy goose . . .'

Then, in a cinematic fade, we are in the company of two naval officers in a Pall Mall club, drinking pink gins and discussing the legend of a white bird flying over the lines of men at the sea's edge. One of them tells how, returning from Dunkirk, his crew sighted the wreckage of a dinghy which had been machine-gunned from the air, with a body half-submerged beside it. On the thwarts was a white bird with black pinions. At that point his ship turns to avoid a German mine, which explodes, destroying the wreckage. When the turmoil of seawater subsides, the white bird is seen flying towards the Essex coast. The Snow Goose is returning to Frith as Rhyader's emissary, to bid her farewell.

Gallico's novella is of course intensely sentimental. Eyebrows were raised in the New York literary world when the eminent publishing house of Alfred Knopf took the story and published it in 1941 (it was published in Britain the same year, and an English critic later adapted an Oscar Wilde quip to write that 'one must have a heart of stone to read *The Snow Goose* without laughing . . .'). And yet in writing a story of Dunkirk in the form of fanciful myth – and in writing it at the darkest of times when London was being bombed and before America had come into the war – Gallico caught the essence of Dunkirk as a turning-point for public resolve.

As I watched the flotilla of Little Ships returning to Ramsgate from their anniversary visit, I thought what an odd assortment they were. There were gentlemen's cruising launches, with brass fittings, teak decks and mahogany hulls. Names like *Sundowner* and *Lazy Days* evoked thoughts of sunlit afternoons upriver from Henley. There were seaside pleasure boats, too, whose names – *New Britannic*, *Miss Margate* – contained memories of candy floss and tea on the sands and trips round the bay. In the harbour there was a paddle-steamer, the *Medway Queen*, whose chunking rhythms would have been heard from Tower Bridge to the North Foreland every day of a pre-war summer, bringing East End trippers to the seaside towns of Essex and Kent.

Even today the idea that these lovely vessels, with their evocative names, had to face the full armoury of Blitzkrieg is incongruous and disturbing – *Sundowner* strafed, *Miss Margate* machine-gunned, *Medway Queen* dive-bombed. Inevitably the public response was outrage: 'They can't do that. It's not right!' And so the British people turned instinctively to their new leader Churchill and asked, 'What must we do?'

It is the incongruity of the Dunkirk story – the mismatch between lyricism and mechanized warfare – which Gallico manages to capture in his 'great' story. A rescue mission undertaken by an outcast, a perilous journey across the sea, a snow-white bird flying above lines of exhausted men, the bird's departure as a spiritual messenger. These are the elements of myth: recounted tales of heroic deeds. And, as Paul Gallico intended, the response of those Americans who first read his fictional account of an historic event in the *Saturday Evening Post* in the autumn of 1940 was overwhelming: 'We must do what we can . . .'

ANDREW JOYNES lives in Ramsgate. His earliest landscape memories are of the Kent shore of the Thames, across the estuary from the marshes of Essex. There the twin towers of the ruined Saxon church of Reculver are silhouetted like Rhyader's lighthouse, and the skeins of wintering geese are like the smoke of bonfires in the winter sky.

Wilderness Years

NICK HUNT

Somewhere in the badlands of Utah is a canyon called Davis Gulch. Centuries ago, the Ancestral Pueblo carved a dwelling in its rock, now inscribed with the words 'NEMO 1934'. This is the last known signature of the vagabond Everett Ruess.

The epithet 'vagabond' was his own, and rarely has the term been so richly deserved. An aspiring artist and writer from a bohemian home in Los Angeles, Ruess set out at the age of 16 on an uncompromising quest to seek out beauty and solitude in the rugged wilderness of the American south-west. Over the next four years he travelled the mountains, deserts and canyon-lands of California, Arizona, New Mexico, Colorado and Utah, alone but for the company of his burro and occasionally a dog. At the age of 20 he disappeared. 'NEMO' might have been a reference to Captain Nemo from *Twenty Thousand Leagues Under the Sea* – another notable seeker of solitude – or else the Greek for 'No Man', as employed by Odysseus.

A Vagabond for Beauty (1983), edited by W. L. Rusho – a federal government employee who became fascinated with Ruess's story – is a compilation of the young man's diary entries, letters to his parents, brother and friends, fragments of prose and poetry, and linoleum landscape prints that he produced in the four years leading up to his disappearance. The book fell into my hands in a suitably serendipitous manner, dropped through my letterbox by a neighbour who knew I was on the look-out for forgotten or unusual travel books.

Everett Ruess, *A Vagabond for Beauty* (1983) · Ed. W. L. Rusho
John Murray · Pb · 304pp · £12.99 · ISBN 9781529376104

Straightaway I was hooked. I've also travelled in solitude, walking for weeks and months on end, but no sooner have I been immersed in true wilderness than I've found myself on the other side, looking back with a bittersweet blend of relief and disappointment. With Ruess there was no looking back. His commitment awed and alarmed me in equal measure.

His first letters home read like snippets from *The Boy's Own Annual* – 'I slept in the middle of a pocket in the sand dunes, building my fire just at dusk . . . I had a jolly time yesterday, tramping up and down the beach' – but one of the joys of this book is witnessing the growth not only of a man but of a writer. He gets better over time, restlessly reworking thoughts and descriptions, honing and improving his prose as if whittling sticks by the campfire. Ruess's type of vagabonding has nothing to do with shiftlessness; he takes his vocation seriously and uses the freedom it affords to apply himself with discipline to the craft, and the daily graft, of writing.

For sure, he can be overindulgent: 'Once more I am roaring drunk with the lust of life and adventure and unbearable beauty.' But it is precisely this lack of filter and this romantic extravagance that result in some of the rawest and most luminous nature writing I've ever read. Ruess really means it. 'As I stalked down from the high perched plain, lightning flashed out from the darkening sky; thunder rolled and reverberated in the narrow canyon,' he writes after witnessing a desert storm. 'A vivid arrow flare of piercing brilliancy struck down at the red cliffs, ricocheting with a sickening whine, like a hurtling shell.' Time and again, the sublime strikes him with the force of lightning, making his prose so electrically charged it can be painful. 'I have seen almost more beauty than I can bear,' he writes in one of his letters. Elsewhere he describes 'such utter and overpowering beauty as nearly kills a sensitive person'.

This acute sensitivity to beauty places Ruess in a long line of ecstatic American experience-seekers from Walt Whitman to Allen Ginsberg and Edward Abbey. Paul Kingsnorth, who wrote the introduction to a new edition of *A Vagabond for Beauty* in 2021, describes him as 'a young, green nature mystic . . . one of those gifted with an aerial through which could flow the divine presence from the Earth itself. This sounds overblown, maybe, but that makes it no less real.'

Despite his predilection for solitude, Ruess was part of West Coast literary and artistic circles that included the poet Robinson Jeffers, the painter Edward Weston ('a very broad-minded man'), and the photographers Ansel Adams and Dorothea Lange, all of whom were moved and inspired by the landscapes of the American West even as man was encroaching on the wilderness. That frontier had long since gone, and the beauty and solitude Ruess described were vanishing even as he wrote about them.

The fact of his youthful disappearance also draws inevitable comparisons with Chris McCandless (a.k.a. Alexander Supertramp) who died in Alaska in 1992, immortalized by Jon Krakauer in *Into the Wild* (1996). Like McCandless, Ruess was dissatisfied with American society, consciously turning his back on the corruption of civilization. He mostly avoided the company of the region's white traders and settlers and – after initial ungracious impressions ('The Navajo live in filth') – increasingly came to admire the Navajos, Hopis, Pueblos and Utes who had lived in these harsh desert landscapes for generations. 'I have often stayed with the Navajos,' he writes in 1934. 'I've known the best of them, and they are fine people. I have ridden with them on their horses, eaten with them and even taken part in their ceremonies. Many are the delightful encounters, and many the exchange of gifts.' He started to learn the Navajo language, attended a traditional Hopi Snake Dance and joined archaeological digs at Ancestral Pueblo sites.

Which brings us to his last known whereabouts at the rock dwelling in Davis Gulch, where he carved that enigmatic inscription before vanishing forever. Of the many theories about his disappearance, two involve Native Americans: perhaps he married a Navajo woman and renounced his white identity; or perhaps he was murdered by Jack Crank, a notorious Navajo outlaw. Alternatively, he was killed by white cattle-rustlers after stumbling on a crime and needing to be silenced. One witness claimed that a local drunk had bragged about shooting the 'goddamned artist kid' and throwing his body in the Colorado River, but no one believed he was capable of it; when W. L. Rusho interviewed this man in 1982 he was suffering from memory loss and seemed to know nothing about it.

Or did Ruess choose to die in solitude and commit suicide? Many of his statements could certainly be interpreted this way. '[H]e who

has looked long on naked beauty may never return to the world,' he wrote, and: 'I'll never stop wandering. And when the time comes to die, I'll find the wildest, loneliest, most desolate spot there is.' Given that he vanished soon afterwards, some have taken him at his word. But what romantically minded adolescent hasn't made similar claims? Unlike many vaga-bonds, Ruess wasn't running away from stifling family expectations or an unhappy home. The letters he exchanged with his family are loving and conversational, and both his parents seemed to be relaxed –

Ansel Adams

even remarkably supportive – about their son's unconventional urge to wander the world alone. It is hard to imagine him killing himself, knowing the heartbreak it would bring. But deserts are strange places. They bring dreams and visions. In the end, we will never know the twists his mind might have taken.

Perhaps the likeliest explanation is that he fell into a ravine or broke his leg in the middle of nowhere, dying of injuries or thirst. His bones would have been carried off by vultures and coyotes. In this, his body would have shared a similar fate to that of Edward Abbey, who asked his eco-anarchist friends to wrap his corpse in an old sleeping-bag and dump it (illegally) in the Sonoran Desert where it would never be found. Seven years before that occurred, Abbey wrote 'A Sonnet for Everett Ruess':

> Hunter, brother, companion of our days:
> that blessing which you hunted, hunted too,
> what you were seeking, that is what found you.

For someone who was so young when he vanished and who never wrote a book, it is remarkable how far Ruess's influence stretches, like a desert shadow.

There is always the danger that Ruess's life story, and the mystery of his disappearance, will overshadow his work, which would be a pity. *A Vagabond for Beauty* is a masterpiece, in the original sense of the word: not the culmination of someone's ambition and the best thing they will ever make, but the piece by which they graduate from being a novice to becoming a master of their chosen craft. Already a master vagabond, Ruess was learning to master his art when his road was cut short by whatever fate befell him. Today, as the wilderness that he loved shrinks ever more rapidly, his unembarrassed worship of nature – and his exuberant love of life – feel more important and more exciting than ever.

> I thought that there were two rules in life – never count the cost, and never do anything unless you can do it wholeheartedly. Now is the time to live.

Rather than 'NEMO', this excerpt from his diary could be his epitaph.

NICK HUNT is the author of three travel books, most recently *Outlandish: Walking Europe's Unlikely Landscapes* (2021), a work of gonzo ornithology and a short-story collection. He is also co-director of the Dark Mountain Project. You can hear him in Episode 42 of our podcast, discussing the travel writing of Patrick Leigh Fermor with Artemis Cooper.

The Tiger under the Bed

MAGGIE FERGUSSON

There are now nearly a million people suffering from dementia in the UK, and I feel as if most of my contemporaries have had some involvement in the affliction either through parents or friends. With my father, it came on very gradually, beginning with odd lapses of memory, repetitions in speech, loss of bearings, groundless anxieties. It was exhausting for my mother, so one afternoon we suggested we take her out for a break and arranged for one of the grandchildren to stay with my father for the few hours she was away. When we told him of this plan, my father was furious: he did not need watching over; he could perfectly well look after himself. Anger is common in the early stages of dementia, and it is fuelled by fear: a mental un-ravelling has begun, and from now on it will only gain momentum.

When Sydneysider Fiona McFarlane set out, in her mid-thirties, to write her first novel, she had witnessed two grandmothers dying with dementia. Wrapping herself in silence – she told nobody what she was working on – she set out to explore dementia 'from the inside'. She was determined not to be sentimental, and instead suc-ceeded in producing a dark, psychological thriller that is suspenseful, shocking and deeply unsettling. No wonder *The Night Guest* (2013) won prizes and was shortlisted for more.

Ruth Field, a former elocution teacher, 75 years old and widowed (kind, gentle Harry is five years dead), lives in an isolated house on the New South Wales coast. Her sons, Jeffrey and Phillip, live in New

Fiona McFarlane, *The Night Guest* (2013)
Sceptre · Pb · 304pp · £9.99 · ISBN 9781444776690

Zealand and Hong Kong respectively, and, as her memory is beginning to slip, she has become rather afraid of them – 'afraid of being unmasked by their youthful authority'. Her grandchildren breathe 'Hello, Nanna' down the phone, but it is clear that they have almost forgotten her: 'She saw them at Christmas and they loved her; the year slid away and she was an anonymous voice, handwriting on a letter, until they arrived at her festive door again.' Ruth's house is so quiet that she can hear if a man whistles to his dogs on the beach below. She has been brought up to believe that boredom is unattractive and loneliness off-putting, so to get herself through the 'gentle, bewildering expanse of the day', she makes mental bargains with herself: 'If she had dinner ready in time for the six o'clock news, both of her sons would come home for Christmas . . .'; if there were fewer than eight small waves before another big one, she would sweep the garden path of sand.

But, in the midst of this carefully maintained order, Ruth is plunged suddenly into perplexity and panic. Waking in the middle of the night, she becomes aware of something large rubbing against her sofa and television. 'Other sounds followed: the panting of a large animal; a vibrancy of breath that suggested enormity and intent; definite mammalian noises, definitely feline, as if her cats had grown in size and were sniffing for food with huge noses.' She is convinced the intruder is a tiger: she had once seen one 'eating at a German zoo, and it sounded just like this: loud and wet, with a low, guttural breathing hum punctuated by little cautionary yelps, as if it might roar at any moment except that it was occupied by food'.

We are used to reassuring people that if something is 'all in the mind', it is not to be feared. Gerard Manley Hopkins knew better:

O the mind, mind has mountains; cliffs of fall
Frightful, sheer, no-man-fathomed. Hold them cheap
May who ne'er hung there.

Fiona McFarlane knows better too. Ruth's encounter with the

tiger is not just a bad dream but a presentiment of evil. In the morning, nothing seems out of place or out of the ordinary except, perhaps, for a yellow taxi idling at the end of her drive. And out of this taxi – the tiger, perhaps, in his daytime garb – steps Frida.

If *The Night Guest* was a film – and it would make a really good one – then the background music for the first couple of chapters would be serene, if a little sad. But once Frida appears on the scene, it becomes hectic, jangling, discordant. She's a nurse, she says, and she's been sent 'by the government: you were on our waiting list and a spot opened up'. She'll start by looking after Ruth for an hour a day.

Frida is large, with hair that she dyes a different shade of brown every few days, and that she wears sometimes loose, sometimes pinned up in complicated coiled braids. She sets about cleaning the house with a reckless, almost warlike energy. The smell of the sea is replaced by the smell of eucalyptus disinfectant – so astringent that Ruth's cats are forced to find new, elevated sleeping places, away from wood and tile. In the morning, before her mood has solidified for the day, Frida acts on whim – kind, or sullen, or genially indignant, or with a Valkyrian aloofness. To the reader, her volatility rings alarm bells. But for Ruth, the easing of loneliness is a priceless boon. When Frida washes her hair, she realizes it's been a long time since anyone had touched her. And the effects of the vigorous housework mean that the tiger fades in her memory. 'A new atmosphere of calm settled over the house; it was cool and clean and noiseless in the night.'

It's a skill well-honed by those who prey on the elderly to find a point of connection that makes them appear kindred spirits. It happened to my grandfather once, when he was sitting on Waterloo Station. A young man, rather a cheeky chappie, settled down next to him and fell into conversation. He persuaded my grandfather – who was slowly losing his memory and reason, like Ruth Field – that they had worked together, years ago, at Barclays Bank. And, guess what? This young man needed some cash, quickly. And guess what . . .

Frida announces that she, like Ruth, grew up in Fiji – well, what do you know? So very soon, her arrival comes to seem not just timely but providential. And she's indefatigable: there is no responsibility she isn't prepared to shoulder – shopping, cooking, cleaning, the sale of Harry's old car. And looking after the money. She confines Ruth to the dining-room while she pores over her bank statements.

Very, very gradually, Ruth begins to sense that something is amiss. Frida begins by addressing her as 'Mrs Field', but this becomes 'Ruth' and then an aggressive 'Ruthie'. Her language morphs from courteous to merrily insolent: 'Don't get your knickers in a twist, Ruthie.' And eventually, Ruth is not even Ruthie, but 'the little old biddy'. When she finally becomes aware that Frida has actually moved into her son Phillip's old bedroom, Ruth knows she must act. She rings her other son, Jeffrey, hoping to tell him in whispers what's afoot. She dials, and the telephone is answered, but all she can hear at the other end is heavy breathing; and then Frida's gusty laughter coming from the room next door.

Anxiety and dread cause the dementia to gallop. At the start of the novel, it is as if someone is tiptoeing gently through the corridors of Ruth's mind turning off the odd switch, but by now lights are fusing violently. When she comes across a box that Frida has crammed with her silver and jewellery, she cannot quite compute what has happened, and why it matters. The tiger returns, and when Frida learns about him she knows exactly how to ratchet up the terror. She takes Ruth, distrait and dishevelled, into town, to the bank, to make a whopping financial transfer. How beady is the bank manager? Will disaster be averted?

Carers can often be far from caring. When my father finally moved into a home, he was miserable. I remember finding him, mid-morning, sitting in front of a swollen Weetabix, while the nurse, heartless and controlling, laid into him for not eating it. Surely, when you get to your mid-eighties, you have the right to decide whether to have your breakfast or not? But then there are the angels. Another nurse working in the home would, during her free time, take Dad down the road in a wheelchair to visit some ponies to whom he had become unaccountably attached.

Fiona McFarlane understands that goodness and cruelty can be inextricably intertwined. As *The Night Guest* reaches its troubling conclusion, treachery and tenderness march together – and the reader experiences at first hand the dementia sufferer's confusion and uncertainty.

I am not going to give away the ending of this page-turning, terrifying novel. But, in place of a spoiler, I'll offer one urgent word of caution. If you have an elderly parent, living alone or with a carer, or even in a care home, be sure to ring her.

MAGGIE FERGUSSON, who is Literary Editor of *The Tablet*, has one daughter who teaches English and another studying it at university. So her bedside reading pile is sky-high. You can also hear her in Episode 11 of our podcast, discussing the work of the Orkney writer George Mackay Brown.

A Stroll down Sinister Street

PAULINE MELVILLE

A while ago on my bookshelves I came across an old copy of *Sinister Street* by Compton Mackenzie. Its cloth binding had faded and the yellowing pages were so fine that I sometimes had to blow on them to open them as I read.

Edmund Gosse believed *Sinister Street* was on a par with *Swann's Way* by Proust, published the same year, 1913. I might well have agreed with him had I ever read any Proust. However, I do know that *Swann's Way* was rejected by many French publishers and Proust was obliged to publish it at his own expense. The reviews were bad. By contrast, *Sinister Street* was greeted with acclaim. One work became a world classic. The other is barely remembered.

Henry James rated Compton Mackenzie as 'the greatest talent of the new generation'. Ford Madox Ford believed *Sinister Street* to be 'possibly a work of real genius'. Evelyn Waugh claimed it was his favourite novel when he was a student and, as young men, both George Orwell and Cyril Connolly admired it. John Betjeman and Max Beerbohm heaped the book with praise. Virginia Woolf, on the other hand, with a more fastidious eye, lumped Compton Mackenzie together with Hugh Walpole as 'the old prostitutes'.

Books are like plants, one outgrowing another and keeping its rival in the shade. This struggle of books against each other is as deadly as all the hidden stranglings and overshadowings of the jungle. Agents, corporate publishers and critics, those literary gardeners,

---

Compton Mackenzie, *Sinister Street* (1913), is out of print, but we can obtain second-hand copies.

weed out lesser plants and spend much time nurturing their prize rose bushes. Their job, in cahoots with the chain bookshops, is to maintain the formal gardens of publishing with all the requisite editing, pruning, topiary and maintenance of pathways. It is in the dusty second-hand bookshops that the neglected plants flourish. That is where the reader, liberated from organized routes into uncharted meadows, is likely to make a rare discovery. And that is where you might find *Sinister Street*.

Edward Montague Compton Mackenzie, born in 1888, came from a family with a long theatrical history. His grandfather, Henry Compton, was considered the best Shakespearean clown of his age, while his parents were actor-managers of the successful Compton Comedy Company which toured the provinces offering a repertoire of Shakespeare, Sheridan and Goldsmith.

All Mackenzie's siblings were connected to the theatre in some way. His sister, Fay Compton, played Ophelia first to John Barrymore's Hamlet and later to John Gielgud's. His brother pursued an acting career in America and his other sisters performed and helped manage the theatre company. This background informed his awareness that the life of theatre folk, those traditional 'rogues and vagabonds', sometimes overlaps with the sort of London riff-raff and ne'er-do-wells found in the later chapters of *Sinister Street*.

In my late teens, working in the theatre, I shared a flat in Soho's Gerrard Street with Compton Mackenzie's niece. That area of theatreland was also home to a variety of scapegraces, artists and small- and big-time gangsters, all mixing together in late-night drinking clubs. In the evening a barrel-organist patrolled the streets, his music bringing a burst of life to the surroundings. A couple of times we visited Fay Compton, then in her seventies and appearing in Turgenev's *A Month in the Country* a few streets away. Wearing her Russian costume, she would come to the stage door to chat and smoke a cigarette until called back on stage. One day my flatmate said, 'Let's go and see Uncle Monty in Edinburgh.' And off we went.

Drummond Place was an elegant Georgian terrace. By this time Compton Mackenzie was in his eighties and the author of some hundred books, including the popular *Whisky Galore*. He was also one of the founding members of the Scottish National Party. He lived with two sisters from the Outer Hebrides, Chrissie and Lillian McSween, wonderful dark-eyed, softly spoken Gaelic speakers. After the death of his first wife he had married Chrissie. She was his wife at the time of our visit. When Chrissie died he married her younger sister Lilli.

Chrissie ushered us into his room where he lay in bed, fully dressed, watching a Western on television. He had a pointed white goatee beard and a good-humoured glint in his eye but his attention remained fixed on the Western and only occasionally alighted on us. That evening we were in the spacious basement kitchen with Chrissie and Lilli. Lilli was in a white flannelette nightie with her hair in curlers. They were trying to sell the house and were expecting prospective viewers. The doorbell rang and Chrissie went upstairs to answer it. Lilli, wanting to stay out of sight, slipped into the large cupboard which also served as a pantry.

Chrissie showed the viewers around the house and then escorted them down to the kitchen. 'As you can see, we have plenty of cupboard space,' she said, flinging open the cupboard door to reveal Lilli standing there in her pale nightie, her black hair twisted into a halo of white rag curlers. 'Och, there you are, Lilli,' she said and shut the cupboard door again. The viewers quickly departed. Later, Uncle Monty came down to roar with laughter as they re-enacted the scene for him. 'Enter Tilburina, stark mad in white satin and the Confidante stark mad in white muslin,' he announced, chortling. Known for his phenomenal memory, he remembered the quote from one of his father's productions of Sheridan's *The Critic*.

They never did sell the house, but Mackenzie scandalized his neighbours by converting the basement kitchen into a hairdressing salon because Lilli had always fancied herself as a hairdresser.

It is difficult to know why the public libraries refused to stock

Sinister Street when it was first published. The novel consists of four books, each one covering a stage in the development of the protagonist Michael Fane, from toddler to boy to student to adult. Mackenzie, in his foreword, says he aimed to keep the reader at the same age as the principal character and so allow us to see the world through his eyes. 'The Prison House' is the first book, a vivid introduction to the world seen through the eyes of a toddler. We experience Michael's daily reality, his interior life, fears and imaginings. When he creeps down at night and peeks through the kitchen door to see his nurse slumped in her chair, speaking loudly and jabbing her finger in the air at the cook, both of them red in the face, he finds their behaviour puzzling. We understand what the child does not, that the domestic staff in the kitchen are blind drunk. From there we progress to the real and imagined horrors of school and the thrill of playing with a friend and saying, 'Maybe it's haunted' or 'Maybe we'll be murdered'. We see his imagination develop term by term.

As a boy Michael is enthralled by a copy of *Don Quixote* with illustrations by Gustave Doré and from then on the spirit of Don Quixote accompanies him everywhere. In fact *Sinister Street* could be seen as a loose reworking of Cervantes' themes, or at least a hat tipped in that direction.

In the second book, 'Classic Education', all the upper-class snobberies of a public school are laid bare, but also the extraordinary depth of scholarship and range of classical knowledge to which pupils were exposed at the time. Mackenzie catches the ever-shifting cloudscape of Michael's adolescent moods. His passionate attachment to his schoolfriend Alan has all the potential for a full-blown homosexual relationship until Michael suddenly becomes ecstatically involved with the Church. In the school holidays there are brief experiments with girls before he is picked up in a bookshop by a gay aesthete and is soon attending Sunday meetings in a room decorated in peacock blue with a group of other exotics who persuade him to read Baudelaire, Verlaine and Mallarmé.

Identity is fluid and volatile at that age. Michael meets and falls head over heels in love with Lily, whom he encounters in Kensington Gardens. Back at school he has an outburst of hatred against the jingoistic attitudes of his classmates during the Boer War. There is something unremittingly tiresome, to modern ears, about the spoken language of the upper classes at the time. 'By Jove, how horribly decent,' doesn't even sound credible to us today, but Compton Mackenzie had a good ear and I suspect it was an accurate reflection of the way in which his contemporaries spoke. Michael rejects the work of G. A. Henty, the imperialist idol of boy readers, and reverts once more to *Don Quixote*. All the way through the book we are shown Michael's literary choices – a reminder that books can be as powerful an influence on developing personalities as genetics, family background or life experience. Then his obsession with Lily is temporarily put aside as he prepares for life at Oxford.

'Dreaming Spires', the third book, encompasses Michael's life at an Oxford college. Dinners, drinking binges, clubs and cricket matches abound. The Bullingdon Club flourishes. Radicals are despised. But we see him progress to an understanding of and sympathy with a fellow student's poverty in an era when some Oxford students chose to sit their Finals in evening dress. He returns once again to *Don Quixote*, accumulates as many editions of the book as possible and goes on impulse to Spain.

The book is laced with satire. On his return from Spain he finds that his mother has joined an association to prevent premature burial:

'My dearest boy, you have no idea of the numbers of people buried alive each year. I have been talking to Dick Prescott about it. I cannot understand his indifference. I intend to devote all my time to it. We are going to organize a large bazaar next season. Banging their heads against the coffins! It's dreadful to think of.'

No wonder Evelyn Waugh liked the novel.

The last book, 'Romantic Education', sees Michael leaving Oxford and diving straight into London's low life, sharing lodgings with thieves and prostitutes whom he feels he has a mission to save. His obsession with an idealized Lily has returned and he is determined to find her, convinced that her appearance on stage in burlesque means that she has sunk to the lowest depths of degradation and he must rescue her. It is Don Quixote and his Dulcinea all over again. When he does find her she is in a clearly and sympathetically portrayed relationship with another woman. Michael briefly manages to lure her away but she returns to her gay lover. I'm not aware of any other female same-sex relationship in a British novel prior to the First World War. Perhaps this was what offended the public libraries. Michael finally accepts the situation. He understands that his chivalry is a form of self-gratification. He declares himself to be an anarchist and sets off for Rome on another quest. By this time his life and Don Quixote's are almost indistinguishable.

Sinister Street is a dense, humorous and intriguing book. Compton Mackenzie had the benefit of a classical education combined with a mountebank's eye for drama and an extraordinary visual memory. Many contemporary novels are written, courtesy of creative writing classes, in the present tense. Their immediacy is as bracing as a slap in the face. *Sinister Street* takes its time, rambles and is meditative and thought-provoking. There are plenty of contemporary highbrow critics who would agree with Virginia Woolf and condemn it as populist, second-rate and trashy. What would Compton Mackenzie say to them were he alive? He might well have chosen a quote from one of his parents' productions of *The Merry Wives of Windsor*: 'Go to hell for an eternal moment or so.'

PAULINE MELVILLE is a British Guyanese writer whose awards include the Guardian Fiction Prize, the Commonwealth Writers' Prize and a Whitbread Prize. Her latest collection of short stories, *The Master of Chaos*, was published in 2021.

Of Mullahs and Magic

TIM BLANCHARD

In the driest of desert towns, Ali Hashemi leaves his bed to say his night prayers. The young man sits in the parched garden of his family's home, an enclosed courtyard that's mostly a place of dust, with a pomegranate tree, a mulberry and a trough of still water. The dawn sky and its brim of lemon-pink colouring passes unnoticed, because Ali is busy with the task set by his teacher.

As he has done for each of his waking hours over the last forty days, Ali repeats the same words over and over: 'There is no might and no power except in God.' The words have become a dirge, a mechanical movement of the lips. 'There is no might and no power except in God.' The repetition and monotony are meant to strip away anything un-necessary, to reduce his awareness to the bare existence of things. That way, only God is left. And it's only now, when both he and the world around him are at their emptiest, whittled down and attenuated, that Ali sees everything differently, in a magical light.

It was not a slowly rising light like that of the dawn; it was not an isolated light like that of the moon or a spotlight. It was everywhere; in fact, it was everything. The pool glowed with light, the garden beds glowed, the sky glowed, the very walls and arches around the courtyard were made of light.

This episode of mysticism lies at the heart of Roy Mottahedeh's

Roy Mottahedeh, *The Mantle of the Prophet: Religion and Politics in Iran* (1985)
Oneworld · Pb · 432pp · £18.99 · ISBN 9781681375182

absorbing story of the making of an Islamic priest, a mullah, in pre-revolution Iran.

It's not really what we, in the West, first think of when Iran is mentioned. Our image of the country is one of archaic ways of thinking and repression, of a place stunted by the Ayatollah Khomeini's 1979 revolution and the ensuing decades of governance mixed up with fundamentalist religion. To us, Iran is the anti-normal: a place where women's rights are restricted, public displays of affection are a criminal act, dogs are unclean and cannot be kept as pets, where the heroes of films must be given the names of Islamic saints (and can never be seen wearing a tie), where teams of censors are employed to scour books for the smallest mention of the inappropriate, like references to wine or pork. Iran does have its own major book fair, but this may be held in only one location: the Grand Mossalah mosque.

Mottahedeh's *The Mantle of the Prophet* (1985) explains how, beneath the forbidding image of the black-robed Ayatollah and a regime of naysaying, there lies a very old, thoughtful, human comedy. I was made to read this wonderful book for a course in cultural history and the sight of its pages still comes with a particular resonance from those student days (the murmur and hiss of a gas fire, the crack of warming metal that's enough to make me want to check my pockets for 50 pence pieces to feed the meter). It was on a reading list – a long, fat reading list – as an example of how cultural history should be done, and it turned out to be an immensely readable and richly peopled excursion into Iranian culture, free from the burden of flashy theorizing.

Mottahedeh was born in America to an Iranian family and attended Quaker schools as a boy, but his homeland remained an irresistible puzzle, rich in romance, and he went on to use part of his first Fellowship award to visit the Middle East, as well as spending time at the University of Cambridge learning Persian and Arabic.

For his book, he drew on many long conversations with Iranians about their lives and experiences, reworking those stories into the composite character of Ali Hashemi and his coming-of-age in the town of Qom, a holy shrine and Iran's highest seat of religious learning. We follow him through the stages of his education – part-awakening, part-disillusion – on a lamp-lit journey, moving from one rough-walled chamber to another, through the innermost workings of Iranian culture.

One of the first surprises is how much of the curriculum of the madrasas, the Islamic schools that some young people attend in addition to their traditional classes, is built on rational argument. The madrasas were set up in the eleventh century – before Europe's universities – as a way of protecting Islam from foreign influence, but they share the same roots: classical logic and reason, grammar and rhetoric. These tools were used to make a good case for the rule of God and his laws, a practical rationality that was at the same time touched with wonder at the magic of existence. The madrasa pupils themselves were known as *talabehs*, meaning 'seekers'. They were not preparing to pass exams, they were on a quest for truth – more like trainee wizards in a world of near-sighted Muggles.

As we follow Ali's progress we discover how everyday Iranian life shaped the character of much Islamic thought. First comes the influence of communal family living: homes without doors; sitting under the same large quilt together on cold evenings; using a tactful code of coughs and heavy footsteps to make sure relatives knew you were coming. It was this lack of privacy that made private, separate moments of contemplation all the more important and affecting.

Then there's the role of gardens in the mental vocabulary of Iranians. Walled gardens: enclosed from the world and its dust and dirt, where any flowers and fruits that grow are a vivid treasure. The Koran itself was one big promise of entry into a 'heavenly garden', and its words weren't seen as a series of arid lessons but rather they had the appeal of myth and legend, as the stories of King Arthur or Middle Earth do for us. The sometimes bloody tales of the Prophet and his descendants felt like living history with a personal significance for individuals and their family line.

An age-old problem for religions has been the demand on ordinary flawed human beings to behave like angels at all times, not just when they're feeling holy. There have to be compromises, and Mottahedeh is particularly good at showing how Iranians approached (and enjoyed) the ambiguities involved, summed up by the Iranian saying: 'God willing, it's a goat.' It comes from a story about a mullah who is late for prayers. Hurrying on his way to the mosque he comes across a dog, soaking wet from a ditch. The dog shakes mud over the mullah's robes. It's his duty under Islamic law to return home and change out of clothes sullied by an unclean creature; but instead the mullah sighs and pretends it might not be a dog after all: 'God willing, it's a goat.' The same approach was taken when it came to a forbidden pleasure like drinking wine. Omar Khayyám was able to write such luxuriantly ripe and lusty poetry about booze ('Let us make up in the tavern for the time we have wasted in the mosque') because ambiguity was so appealing and so healthy. To satisfy other sensual appetites, mullahs were able to arrange a strictly temporary marriage in exchange for filling out the right forms and a fee.

Devotion to Islam in the twentieth century became a kind of consolation. Successive secular governments in Iran had brought in technical expertise from Britain, France and America in order to modernize the country. Increasing numbers of young people, and a greater proportion than in any other nation, were being sent to the West for a university education in order to train as engineers and scientists. It came to feel like a capitulation to Western culture, a sense of defeat known as 'West-stricken-ness'. By the 1960s many more of the country's secular intellectuals were returning to the embrace of Islam, tired of seeing their children indoctrinated into what was still an alien culture. Even if they didn't and couldn't believe in the dogma, Islam worked for them as a native folklore. Cassette tapes of Ayatollah Khomeini's sermons became a fashionable acquisition, a signal of their modish rebellion. So the rise of a religious state didn't come about through force, the success of a strategic campaign, lobbying or political shenanigans, but because there was an emotional surge of support from the mass of Iranians. 'It had been a victory of the word,' wrote Mottahedeh.

Combining religion with politics on a day-to-day level of expediency, though, led to an unfortunate mangling of Iran's delicate, messy cultural poetry. There was a need to put an end to the ambiguity, to start fixing laws and punishing offenders; to stop the flow of more open-ended learning and thinking in order to enforce rules of behaviour. A dog was a dog, a goat was a goat.

Reading the book again made me wonder, though, how different we really are from the narrow-minded regimes we tend to criticize. We assume we're right in just the same way that they do. We want to bulldoze through in the name of 'modern' rights and freedoms (it's good for business, after all), without stopping to consider the subtleties, depths and qualities that other cultures (and communities of people) might have.

By the end of the book, Ali Hashemi knows that becoming a mullah isn't much of an end in itself, he's not 'made it' professionally or booked himself an upgrade in heaven. If anything, it means a more fragile faith, more doubt and scepticism. There is no certain knowledge to rely on, only a cycle of book-reading, a slow evolution of thought, an ebb and a flow; and that was the only way to understand God – whatever that term might mean.

When anti-Shah protests begin to bubble over in the streets of Tehran, a friend asks Ali what he would do with his money if he needed to withdraw it from the bank quickly, and his answer is unequivocal: 'Now and always – buy books.'

TIM BLANCHARD was a choirboy at St Mary's church in Luton in the late 1970s. He never really got the hang of walking in a cassock at the same time as singing and holding a candle.

Before Darkness Fell

IAN THOMSON

In the summer of 1939, my grandfather Erich Haugas took part in an international agricultural conference a thousand miles away in Budapest. He was 38 and his professional pride was flattered. As a

Erich Haugas and his sisters Benita and Ella

chemist he was in charge of the Dairy Export Control Station laboratory in the Estonian capital of Tallinn. To his untravelled eyes this was the trip of a lifetime: Budapest was the last stretch of Western 'civilization' before the East and the closest to a west European capital that many east Europeans would get. No direct train went to Budapest: my grandfather had to take three trains through Latvia, Polish-occupied Lith-

uania, Poland and the Nazi vassal state of Slovakia: a round trip of 2,300 miles. Europe was very close to war, but to my grandfather the rumours of war were just that: rumours.

Eric Ambler, 'unquestionably our best thriller writer', according to Graham Greene, published his fifth and perhaps finest spy novel that fateful year of 1939. In pages of atmospheric prose *The Mask of Dimitrios* (published in America as *A Coffin for Dimitrios*) anatomizes the heart of Europe's darkness on the eve of war. In it, an English

---

Eric Ambler's *Uncommon Danger* (1937), *Epitaph for a Spy* (1938), *Cause for Alarm* (1938) and *The Mask of Dimitrios* (1939) are all available as Penguin paperbacks at £9.99 each.

university lecturer and writer, Charles Latimer, travels to Istanbul by train via Sofia sometime in the late 1930s in order to gather material for a novel, only to find himself entangled in the affairs of a Greek criminal, Dimitrios Makropoulos. Ambler's storytelling powers and mastery of suspense were at their height. The writing combines the precision of a chemist and engineer – two professions Ambler deeply admired – with the sense of melodrama he inherited from his parents, who were music-hall artists based in south-east London.

My grandfather was never caught up in an Ambler-like mesh of intrigue abroad but his journey to Hungary took him through a mass of shifting European frontiers electric with future troubles. In 1937 and 1938, Ambler wrote a string of espionage thrillers – *Uncommon Danger*, *Epitaph for a Spy*, *Cause for Alarm* – that unfold along the disputed frontiers of pre-war Europe. Sensing the gathering emergency, he cut his characters adrift in a world shadowed by Nazi and Stalinist terror. Chemists, commercial photographers, export travellers, engineers, journalists: Ambler's are lower-middle-class anti-heroes far removed from the hunting-shooting-fishing brigade depicted by Sapper and John Buchan. Often they have foreign blood or are not wholly British. Josef Vadassy, the refugee teacher wrongly accused of espionage in *Epitaph for a Spy*, was born in Hungary and has a Yugoslav passport. ('If you don't mind my saying so, you don't look British,' he is told.) Spy novels had existed before Ambler, but few had described the treachery and double-dealing inherent in the trade in a Europe that was about to detonate.

*

With a suitcase packed for a two-week absence, my grandfather arrived at the Baltic Station in Tallinn in the early hours of a July morning. He surely was filled with nervous anticipation. Latimer himself feels a sense of unease when he boards his train for Sofia. Frontiers have a dynamism of their own in Ambler's spy fiction and set off a reflex of anxiety. The Tallinn platform was buzzing with the excitement of an imminent departure. The Estonian State Railways train to Budapest was made up of smart dark green carriages, and in the restaurant car the tables lit by small lamps were already laid for breakfast. The purser showed my grandfather to his sleeping-car compartment.

The station clock struck the hour – 9 a.m. – and the train began to move. Passengers adjourned to the dining-car. My grandfather was still at breakfast when the train reached the Estonian university town of Tartu (where, in 1901, he had been born to a minor Tsarist functionary). At Valga four hours later the train stopped. Valga was on the Estonian-Latvian border and rife with smuggling. Estonian police in grey fatigues came down between the lines with leashed dogs. They made a list of all the passengers – names, nationalities – and searched some of their luggage. A number of Polish and Lithuanian nationals got on. Szepsel Berkman, an accountant, was on his way to see Jewish relatives in Vilnius in Polish Lithuania. Jews were not popular. Admiral Horthy, the anti-Semitic and anti-Slav regent of Hungary, had allied himself with Hitler in the hope of reclaiming land lost to Hungary after the First World War. With the Führer's help Horthy had already recovered parts of southern Slovakia and Subcarpathian Ruth (the birthplace, incidentally, of Andy Warhol's mother Julia Warhola). In Ambler's espionage, European power-politics are a dirty game where a nation's fate is often decided in the boardroom and political ideologies are determined by the dictators.

Belching steam, the train edged backwards out of Valga through a level crossing. The Latvian border – a stretch of no man's land called the Neutral Zone – was closed off by a barrier of red and white, the Latvian colours. An official with the Red Lion and Silver Griffin of Latvia on his cap stamped my grandfather's passport and three hours later the train pulled into the Latvian capital of Riga. Columns of steam rose from the waiting engine while porters loaded the guard's van with crates of food and alcohol. From Riga the train proceeded to Daugavpils (Dvinsk under the Tsars). Daugavpils had a rich Jewish culture (the American painter Mark Rothko was born there in 1903)

but the station would soon facilitate the indus-
trial horror that was Hitler's war on Polish
Jewry. Ambler's most politically engaged thriller,
Cause for Alarm (1938), set in Fascist Italy on the
eve of Mussolini's 1938 legislation against Italian
Jews, was written in response to the threat posed
to Europe by anti-Semitic populist political
movements.

Before long the train had reached Zemgale, the
border point between southern Latvia and Poland. The
station, built in 1922, today serves as a Roman Catholic
church but in my grandfather's day it was a vital crossroads.
Unsurprisingly, Zemgale stood on contested land. In 1920, after seiz-
ing a sliver of Lithuania, Poland had confiscated part of Latvia's
border close to Zemgale. As a result, violence was mounting daily
between Lithuanian and Polish nationals. From Zemgale the train
settled to its rhythm, passing through the Polish border station of
Turmonolo (now Turmantas in Lithuania), a main transit point for
Kharkiv in Soviet Ukraine.

From Turmonolo my grandfather arrived at Vilnius, the *de jure*
capital of Lithuania, which Lithuania had surrendered to Poland in
1922 following the Polish-Lithuanian War that broke out after the
First World War. (Vilnius was 'Wilno' to the Poles.) Before long the
train was moving across western Belarus and then it arrived at
Bialystok, the largest city in north-eastern Poland, situated today in
the so-called Suwalki Gap, a 60-mile-long strip of Poland and
Lithuania straddled to the west by Putin's Russia and to the east by
Belarus under Putin's dictator ally Lukashenko. If there is to be a
Third World War, say the experts, it may flare up in this region.

Warsaw approached and in their sleeping compartments the passengers stirred. A mass of blast furnaces and ancient castles rose along
the line. At Warsaw Central the passengers got off and changed
trains. The new train went all the way to Athens via Istanbul (where,

we learn early on in *The Mask of Dimitrios*, Makropoulos has been murdered and his body dumped in the Bosporus). During the three-hour wait at Warsaw under the station's glass vaulting my grandfather enquired at the Slovak embassy if Slovak visas were required of Estonian nationals. The embassy said they were not. As a newborn republic, Slovakia felt a kinship with Estonia, which had declared independence from post-Tsarist Russia in 1918.

On 8 July – day two of my grandfather's journey across Ambler country – the frontiers of Poland and Slovakia converged at the Polish station of Czaca on the edge of Nazi-occupied Czech lands. Strikingly, the two Polish borders my grandfather had crossed thus far – at Zemgale and Czaca – were the result of inter-war nationalist annexations. In the autumn of 1938, while Ambler was at work on *Epitaph for a Spy*, Poland had grabbed a part of Slovakia close to Czaca, an annexation of Czech-governed territory that amounted to an attack on fellow Slavs and appeared to put Warsaw on the same low moral level as Nazi Berlin. The Polish government was now actively pursuing right-wing anti-Semitic policies of varying toxicity.

Sunlight flooded the carriage as Polish officials boarded the train and examined my grandfather's papers. They stamped a circular blue CZACA in them before the train inched forwards across the frontier into Slovakia, in what was once the Czech Republic. Everything was quiet at Čadca. In this wolf-harbouring part of the Carpathian Mountains with its hazel spinneys and flower-filled summer meadows the Slovak people lived under Hitler's shadow. Everyone in Slovakia – even Jews – had a swastika in their passports. Slovakia had allied itself gratefully to Hitler on its secession from Czechoslovakia in March 1939; by the time Ambler finished *The Mask of Dimitrios* the Nazis had marched into Prague and effectively dismembered Czechoslovakia. Slovakia was poised to become the gateway of the new Nazi empire into the Balkans and the Occupied East. Hundreds of miniature red, white and black swastika flags fluttered along the Čadca station platform.

The Slovak customs police with their red shoulder boards and peaked caps greeted my grandfather with a 'Heil Hitler'. Did he give the Nazi salute in return? (One of the first decisions any foreign traveller had to make in Axis Europe in 1939 was whether or not to outstretch the arm in fascist greeting.) Soon afterwards the train approached the Hungarian border station of Losonc (today Lučenec, in southern Slovakia), where passengers had to disembark and queue up outside a customs shed. Hungary was still nominally a monarchy and a Royal Hungarian policeman looked through my grandfather's paperwork with slow deliberation before stamping *M.KIR* – 'Kingdom of Hungary' – in his passport. For a fee of 50 fillérs (the 'penny' of interwar Hungary) he was granted a Hungarian visa 'posteriorly' as he had neglected to secure one back in Tallinn.

The wheels thudded along the tracks towards Budapest. The Danube flowed alongside, less a waterway than a mirror reflecting vanished Austro-Hapsburg lands. In its east-west meander from Bavaria to the Black Sea the Danube had united under the double-headed eagle Turkish Tartars, Russians, Ukrainians, Serbs, Bulgarian Muslims, Jews, Roma and Russian Old Believers: East to West, Muslim to Christian. Few wished for the Hapsburg empire's return yet Hitler and Stalin between them were about to unleash a viciousness far greater than anything the German-Hungarian rulers in their Vienna fastness could have dreamed of. Jewish communities would disappear overnight as monarchical semi-tolerance was replaced by totalitarian intolerance. Fascism had become Europe's new 'sacred religion', as Ambler wrote in *Cause for Alarm*. Something new was beginning in the Danubian heartlands: quite what, no one yet knew.

After Szob the couplings strained and my grandfather's train at last pulled into Budapest-Keleti.

The station, all elaborate gilt and stucco with marble Germanic Hapsburg nymphs and satyrs under the architraves, had no equivalent in the Baltic. After Tallinn, everything looked gigantic. People dashed frantically down the platform to secure seats for Istanbul and other east-west connections. Over the platform hung a smell of charcoal smoke and fried paprika pods: unfamiliar Magyar smells. My grandfather took a taxi to Pest on the Danube's left bank where he unpacked at the Danube Palace Hotel.

Next day the conference opened beneath the Renaissance dome of the Hungarian Parliament building. Delegates were welcomed over champagne and platters of Danube sturgeon roe. As Estonia's representative my grandfather had to shake hands with Admiral Horthy but what he made of the Magyar dictator is not recorded. He gave a series of talks on dairy chemistry and food preservation. He visited the great Hungarian plains beyond Budapest and swam in the Gellért thermal baths near the Franz Josef Bridge where for the first time he became aware of Budapest's huge non-Magyar component – the so-called 'nationalities', the Serbs, Croats, Romanians and Slovaks who made up half of Hungary's population. *The Mask of Dimitrios* is haunted by the collapse of the Hapsburg, Ottoman and Tsarist empires and by the populations displaced by war from Odesa, Kyiv, Smyrna and Istanbul. Ambler had brought the political thriller to maturity in post-imperial Europe.

By the time Erich Haugas came home to Tallinn in late July 1939 the Second World War was less than two months away. The Baltic city with its medieval ramparts and quaint cobbled streets seemed so far removed from the tide of world events as to be almost unreal. The hotels were full of tourists, there was a fever of entertaining and drinking in the nightclubs. Darkness was about to fall on the unhappy continent of Europe.

IAN THOMSON is a writer and journalist. He is currently working on a book for Faber on the Baltic during the Second World War.

Fertile Ground

URSULA BUCHAN

When I was a child, I was fascinated by much that was American. I particularly enjoyed Californian grapefruit, chewing gum, Westerns, *Stuart Little* and the covers and cartoons of the *New Yorker*. A dozen enormous grapefruit would arrive in a box every Christmas, sent by a cousin of my mother's, while chewing gum ('that dreadful American habit!' according to my teachers) was forbidden, so its consumption was deliciously furtive. We watched thrilling Westerns on our black-and-white television at weekends and I delighted in the sublime children's story *Stuart Little*, never thinking that a tale about the mouse-child of a New York couple was at all an odd idea. Most of all, I loved the cartoons in the *New Yorker*, a magazine I fell upon every time we visited my aunt and uncle. They had lived for some years in the States in the 1950s, when my uncle was Washington correspondent of the *Observer*. These enlightened relatives even owned a large cupboard that was decorated with *New Yorker* covers.

I wonder now whether the memory of the *New Yorker* and *Stuart Little* was the reason why, some years ago, I bought a second-hand copy of *Onward and Upward in the Garden* by Katharine S. White. Or perhaps it was simply a desire to prove my Anglocentric friends wrong when they airily dismissed American garden writers as not being a patch on their British counterparts. Whatever the cause, I am

---

Katharine S. White's *Onward and Upward in the Garden*, edited and with an introduction by E. B. White (1979), and *Two Gardeners: A Friendship in Letters*, edited by Emily Herring Wilson (2002), are out of print, but we can obtain second-hand copies.

glad I did, for I found a sympathetic writer, one with a keen eye, a refreshing rigour and an attractively dry sense of humour.

Onward and Upward in the Garden is an anthology of fourteen long *New Yorker* articles, collected and introduced by Katharine's husband E. B. White, a brilliant essayist and the author of my much-loved *Stuart Little*, as well as that other children's classic, *Charlotte's Web*. Katharine had spent most of her working life as fiction editor for the *New Yorker* and these articles were published between 1958 and 1970. She died in 1977, and *Onward and Upward* appeared two years later, a tender homage to her talents and personality by a bereft husband.

Katharine Sergeant came from an impeccably upper-crust East Coast family, both her parents being descendants of families that had come to America from England in the seventeenth century. Her childhood was spent in Brookline, Massachusetts, close to Boston and down the road from Harvard's Arnold Arboretum. She graduated from Bryn Mawr College in 1914. Every account I have read of her time at the *New Yorker* mentions how meticulous she was as an editor. (Her discussions with John Updike on punctuation, and in particular the dash and the colon, became the stuff of legend.) She married, first, Eric Angell and bore him two children, one of whom, Roger, would also become a fiction editor at the *New Yorker*.

In 1925, she persuaded Harold Ross, the founder of the recently launched magazine, to take on E. B. ('Andy') White. She left Eric Angell for White and they married in 1929 and had a son. The celebrated essayist and the discerning fiction editor must have made a powerful celebrity couple in the years before and after the Second World War. It is easy to forget, these days, just how influential White and the *New Yorker* were in shaping American literary culture, in particular giving space and encouragement to writers such as John O'Hara, Mary McCarthy, Vladimir Nabokov and John Updike.

Adam Begley, the author of a biography of Updike, describes the relationship between editor and writer:

Ten years after her death in 1977, [Updike] wrote about the warmth she conveyed, 'her aristocratic sureness of taste', her 'instinctive courage and integrity', her 'ethical ardor'; he also stressed that her 'good humor and resilience were as conspicuous as her dignity and (when provoked) her hauteur'.

In 1933, the Whites bought a farm at North Brooklin on the coast of Maine, where they weekended until 1957, when they moved there permanently. This was where Katharine did her gardening or, more accurately, garden overseeing, for her health was not good and much of the practical work was done by someone else. The articles she wrote coincided with a golden age of 'chatty' garden books in Britain – although 'chatty' is too dismissive a word for the often amusing, always illuminating, ruminations of intelligent, hard-working amateur gardeners – but there were, at the time, very few American writers who could match them.

In truth, Katharine White's *New Yorker* pieces are not straightforward gardening articles but rather extended reviews of books and nursery catalogues; however, much horticultural and personal information is imparted in the process, making me fervently grateful that I live on an island with a temperate maritime climate, for it is a much easier place in which to garden than the north-east coast of America. She used these reviews to tell tales of her childhood and her gardening life, and to round up other books on the subject under review which had appealed to her.

She was in thrall to the romance of nursery and seed catalogues, with all the promise they hold out for a more colourful and satisfactory garden future. I am glad that she did not see the day when the Internet quite destroyed that romance. She was a woman of decided opinions: she had a particular down on plants that had been made stunted and vulgar by breeders, zinnias being an egregious example. Her first ever article was entitled 'A Romp in the Catalogues' and it must have given the magazine's readers quite a jolt. I wonder what the eminent nurseryman David Burpee thought of her strictures on the names of antirrhinums:

> 'Snaps' is Burpee's word, not mine. I detest the cozy flower abbreviations. 'Mums' is probably the most repellent of the lot, unless it is 'Glads', but 1959 gave us a new nasty – 'Dels', for the lordly delphiniums.

And here she is on the subject of *Gladiolus*:

> Half my prejudice [against gladioli] may lie in this flower's uneuphonious name, with its awkward plural, and especially in its horrid nickname. I can not be glad about glads.

She loved the wildflowers she knew in Maine, writing affectionately of the distinctly euphoniously named bloodroot, black cohosh, Dutchman's breeches, ladies' slipper, cardinal flower, cat tail and Turk's cap lily. I particularly enjoyed her description of picking fragrant water lilies from a small boat on Lake Chocorua as a girl. It is interesting to note that already, in the 1960s, she was expressing unease at the accelerating loss of biodiversity in America. In that regard she was ahead of her time.

I am not sure that I can entirely articulate the appeal of a book that describes nurseries of which I have never heard and which probably no longer exist, with descriptions of plants that I don't know, and a gardening climate and conditions so different to my own. I think it is because Katharine White seems to value her readers and wishes to communicate with them – to share a joke about the eccentricity of gardening folk, but also to elicit our admiration for their fundamental decency and skills. And, for a woman who earned her living making something of other people's words, it is not surprising that, when there were no longer Updikes or Nabokovs to encourage, she should turn to the devisers of catalogues.

She maintained that she found writing very difficult, and her husband confirmed this in the book's introduction:

Katharine's act of composition often achieved the turbulence of a shoot-out. The editor in her fought the writer every inch of the way; the struggle was felt all through the house. She would write eight or ten words, then draw her gun and shoot them down. This made for slow and torturous going. It was simple warfare – the editor ready to nip the writer before she committed all the sins and errors the editor clearly foresaw.

Paradoxically, 'Her letters flowed naturally from her in a clear and steady stream, a warm current of affection, concern, and eagerness to get through to the mind of the recipient.' This I can confirm for, in the process of researching this piece, I discovered that there was a published compilation of more than 150 letters between Katharine White and Elizabeth Lawrence, a distinguished gardening writer from Charlotte, North Carolina. They had formed a strong, touching and enlivening epistolary friendship, beginning when Elizabeth wrote Katharine a fan letter after she had read 'A Romp in the Catalogues'. Elizabeth Lawrence, the professional, gave much useful advice to Katharine White, the amateur, especially widening her knowledge of nurseries and plants, and describing gardening conditions in a very different climate from that of Maine. *Two Gardeners: A Friendship in Letters* was sensitively edited by Emily Herring Wilson and published in 2002 by Beacon Press. It is a delight to read, because the two women have plainly recognized in each other a kindred spirit, despite the difference in their gardening circumstances. Elizabeth, according to Katharine, was 'a classicist, and can cite Virgil and the English poets as freely as she does Gertrude Jekyll and Jane Loudon'. She wrote to her, 'You are my candidate always for an American who writes on gardening subjects as well as the English do.' That makes two of them.

URSULA BUCHAN is sorry that she was born both too late and in the wrong place to meet these two remarkable women. You can hear her in Episode 9 of our podcast, discussing the history of garden writing.

The Stuff of Nightmares

SAM LEITH

'You remember me . . .' Whoosh. Those three words still send a little thrill of terror down my spine. I don't think I'm the only adult for whom, when they look back on their childhood reading, the books that scared them are remembered with a particular intensity. Just as childhood nightmares stay with us, so do stories – some of them seeming quite innocent to adults – which wobbled some fragile pillar of childhood security.

Dracula, which I read far too young, still sticks with me: the spider walking outside the castle; the horrible flush on the monster's face – 'the eyes were open and stony, but without the glassiness of death' – when Harker first finds him dormant in his coffin. And Ray Bradbury's superbly spooky short stories, 'Skeleton' most of all. The Great Long Red-Legg'd Scissor-Man in *Struwwelpeter*. The ginger-bread house in *Hansel and Gretel*. And, above all of these, *Grinny* – in which the three words with which I began this piece take on a special significance.

Grinny, published in 1973, is a children's novel by Nicholas Fisk that has long been out of print. The narrator is 11-year-old Timothy Carpenter, who lives an ordinary suburban existence with his father and mother and 7-year-old sister Beth. In the very first paragraph, the doorbell rings and he answers it. On the step, 'with two ginor-mous trunks', is a little old lady. 'I'm your Great Aunt Emma,' she says. 'You must be Tim.'

Nicholas Fisk, *Grinny* (1973), is out of print, but we can obtain second-hand copies.

Here is how she is described in Tim's diary, the entries in which make up the substance of the narrative:

> She is rather a queer old party. Very short, with a hat with a veil, and gloves, and a way of smiling vaguely. Her teeth are very good (false?) and she is very neat. Her shoes hardly have creases in them over the instep, as if she never walked, yet she is quite spry considering her age and soon she and Mum were chattering away about the journey and so on.

While Tim and Beth are disconcerted by this unexpected arrival, whose name has never before been mentioned, their parents take her in immediately. One moment Tim's mother is asking: '*Who?* Great Aunt who?' Then the queer old party says: 'You remember me, Millie!' At once, Millie exclaims: 'Great Aunt Emma! Oh do come in, you must be freezing. Tim, help with the luggage.'

Great Aunt Emma – or GAE as she is abbreviated in Tim's diary – is ensconced in the spare bedroom. Without discussion or warning, and with no end in sight, she is now part of the family. And it soon becomes clear that there is something very strange indeed about her. But even as Tim and Beth come, bit by bit, first to notice and then (though only ever partly) to understand her strangeness, their parents remain completely oblivious. Even now, as Tim writes in his retrospective Introduction, 'Of course, I can never talk to my father and mother about Aunt Emma – they quite literally *would not hear me.*'

One of the compelling oddities of *Grinny* is the way in which it's framed. As Tim's Introduction explains, the diary entries that make up the main body of the text have been published at his urging by his writer friend Nicholas Fisk. Tim, now the book has been published, is 15: 'I was too young to have done anything about Aunt Emma when she was with us because I was never sure what it all meant and even when everything got frightening and sinister I could neither have proved anything nor gone to someone for help.' Here, in compressed form, is the stuff of childish nightmares – that combination of impotence (you're just a child; nobody will believe you) and incomprehension in the face of a threat.

But here, too, is that sense – used to similarly disturbing effect in adult horror fiction including *Dracula, Frankenstein* and Mark Z. Danielewski's *House of Leaves* – of the authenticity of what in film shorthand is sometimes called 'found footage'. We're exposed, unmediated, to the story unfolding in contemporary documents in real time. There's no reassuring sense of an author making it up or shaping the story to make it make sense.

And the diaries of this 11-year-old boy – bright, a little pretentious, loquacious, slangy, telegraphic – sound like the diaries of any 11-year-old boy. Tim's bickering and competitive relationship with Beth, and his scorn at the way his friend Mac likes to ingratiate himself with her, will be absolutely relatable to any reader with a sibling. He's an 11-year-old boy who is proud of his relationship with an author, and who is even trying to shape himself as a writer: 'I find I am writing very slangily. Various uses of "chuffed" in this entry and lazy use of "and". *Memo: if you are going to write this much, even in a diary, you might as well write it right.*' The gathering horror of the situation jars, especially at first, with the tone – which is at times reminiscent of P. G. Wodehouse or even Molesworth. The pages are filled with memos-to-self, rhetorical questions in parentheses, daily trivia, multiple exclamation marks, tags like 'Etc., etc.', and abbreviations.

I think that's one of the things that makes it more rather than less disturbing. It isn't full of creaking Gothic furniture, or the foreshadowing and foreboding that make lesser horror stories scream, paragraph by paragraph, that they are horror stories. And Great Aunt Emma's oddities are, at first, just that: oddities. Why does she seem to be nervous around electricity? How can she smoke untipped Gauloise after untipped Gauloise? Is that connected to Beth's growing unease at the fact that – under the fag smoke – she doesn't smell of anything at all? How come – such a sinister detail, because so unexpected and incidental and unexplained – the tops of her shoes are uncreased? Beth nicknames her 'Grinny' because of her incessant disconcerting smile.

Grinny always finds ways of deflecting questions about her own life. And she asks odd questions – to the extent that nobody is quite sure whether she's making a joke or not. Is she being funny when, after the children mention a championship-winning 'cast-iron conker', she seems to expect it to be made, literally, of iron? When she breaks in on the family bathing naked in the swimming pool they nickname 'Muscle Beach', she seems oblivious to the idea that they might be embarrassed by being seen undressed.

Beth becomes convinced that Grinny is not human – and her conviction is cemented when Grinny slips on ice and breaks her wrist. Here's Tim's diary entry:

'The skin was gashed open but there was no blood. The bones stuck out but they were not made of real bone – they were made of shiny steel!'

I have these words right. Beth did say what I have written. I am quite certain about asking her what sort of bones, what sort of steel and so on. Her answers were, that the steel was silvery shiny and that the bones looked smaller than proper bones – more like umbrella ribs. When I asked her what umbrella ribs look like, she answered (correctly) that they are made of channels of steel, not solid rods like knitting needles. She said that GAE's bones were in 'little collections' of these steel ribs and that the skin had been torn by a few of the ribs breaking away from a main cluster and coming through the skin.

What makes *Grinny* so effective is its extreme oddness and the specificity of that oddness. We are in the territory of what Freud called the *unheimlich*. The root of that word – *heimlich*, homely – points to why it is so disturbing in this context. Grinny is inside the home, inside the place that in most children's literature is the locus of comfort and security, and which children leave to have their adventures and return to at the end. And here the adults, who in most children's literature are the guarantors of the home's comfort and security, are no use at all. Grinny has them hypnotized.

Did you ever have one of the kind of recurring dreams where you are running from monsters, and you reach the safety of your mother and father – and then they reach down to their chins, and slowly pull off their masks . . . ? Yes, me too.

As the children come to realize with deepening terror, Grinny is the trial balloon for an alien invasion. When they see a flying saucer out of the window one night, and rush to wake her, it becomes clear that her sleeping habits are . . . unconventional.

> Grinny was lying flat on her back on the bed, with her arms by her side above the covers. She was rigid and still, like a corpse or an Egyptian mummy. But she was luminous. There was even a faint glow through the bedclothes.
>
> I went closer – I wasn't frightened yet – and saw another thing: her eyes were wide open. She was staring at the ceiling, staring at nothing. And her eyes were lit up from inside. Like water when you put the lens of a lit torch in it. Her mouth was open. She was grinning. I don't mean she was making the movement of smiling, I mean her mouth was set in a grin. And from her open mouth I thought I heard a slight fluttering, twittering sound.

That fluttering, twittering sound – which in my imagination resembles the unworldly blips and squawks of a tape drive or a dial-up modem – is the language that the children come to call 'Grinnish'. When Grinny is disconcerted or under extreme stress, her speech starts to break down and her English is interspersed with Grinnish.

The story gets stranger still, as the children learn to fight back. They discover that they can scramble Grinny's circuits with what they call 'eyes right': a trick of keeping your eyes fixed a foot or so to one side of her head, rather than looking at her directly. It is nowhere explained why this works or really how they hit upon it. Again, we are in the territory, I think, of the logic of dreams – and of that atavistic space in which barely understood home-made magic is used to keep the illegible terrors of the universe at bay. It connects, in my mind, with the magic that the children use to fight the monster in that other great book about childhood terror (though emphatically not one for children), Stephen King's *It*.

The fact that so little is spelled out seems to me to explain why the novel is so terrifying. We know Grinny is a threat, an existential threat – not only to the planet but, more viscerally, to the safe order of childhood experience itself. But she can't be folded into a knowable scheme of the universe. We have a series of irreducible nightmare images – a bloodless wound; a sheaf of umbrella-spokes; a watery light in the eyes; luminous teeth; uncreased shoes; and a dull metal 'torch thing . . . as busy and unstoppable as a rat, never pausing from its nibblings and humped-up scurryings and lunges and tugs'. And we have an untranslatable shrill inhuman language, counterposed (in a book where language is to the fore) to the oh so human language of Tim's diary entries.

Forgotten? Why, no, Nicholas Fisk: I remember you.

SAM LEITH is literary editor of the *Spectator* and the author of a number of books including *You Talkin' to Me? Rhetoric from Aristotle to Trump and Beyond* and *Write to the Point: How to Be Clear, Correct and Persuasive on the Page*. He's currently researching a history of children's literature to be published by Oneworld in 2024.

Having the Last Word

ANTHONY QUINN

According to a paperback column in the *Daily Telegraph* (15 August 1988) I greatly admired Penelope Lively's *Moon Tiger* (1987) and thought its closing pages 'among the most moving I have read in years'. I wasn't alone; the novel had already won the rather more significant distinction of the Booker Prize the year before, marking the high point of Lively's much-honoured career in both adult and children's fiction. So why, given my proclaimed enthusiasm, did I not read another word of hers for more than thirty years? Impossible to explain, though I made good the deficit recently, having spent the first lockdown reading about a dozen of her books in close succession.

I began with her wonderful memoir of old age, *Ammonites and Leaping Fish* (2013), in which the author notes, 'The body may decline, may seem a dismal repetition of what went before, but the mind has a healthy continuity, and some kind of inbuilt fidelity to itself, a coherence over time . . .' Claudia Hampton, heroine-historian of *Moon Tiger*, is an old woman in decline, dying of stomach cancer in a hospital bed, yet her mind remains as sharp and her temperament as cussed as they were in her prime. 'I am writing a history of the world', she announces, and as a maverick of her trade she intends to provoke – to shock. Maybe she can tell it from the point of view of the 'primordial soup', of a crustacean, or of an ammonite: 'An ammonite with a sense of destiny'.

Happily for the reader Claudia chooses not to go full Jurassic and

Penelope Lively, *Moon Tiger* (1987)

Penguin · Pb · 224pp · £8.99 · ISBN 9780241973684

instead concentrates upon the life *she* has lived, and the people she has known and loved – and lost. *Moon Tiger* still manages to be a work of formal, and formidable, sophistication. It kaleidoscopes personal history, darts from first person to third, hopscotches in and out of time. Scenes are replayed with a different emphasis or in a different voice. Claudia accepts the slippery nature of her project, and will allow others to speak, to give their side of the story – 'Except that of course I have the last word. The historian's privilege.' So she begins in childhood on the Dorset coast fossil-hunting with her brother Gordon, 'an unkempt, unruly pair', while on their mother's dressing-table stands a photograph of their father, a fatality of the Somme, 'picked off by history'.

As a narrator she proves to be strong meat: arrogant, abrasive, opinionated, never afraid of being disliked. She believes she has people worked out, like Jasper, her ambitious, selfish lover; her plump, submissive sister-in-law, Sylvia; her only child, Lisa, apparently stolid and disapproving of her flamboyant mother. But in one of the novel's quicksilver shifts of perspective we find that Lisa isn't the dull daughter we imagine her to be, that she too has a hinterland unsuspected by the parent. We are mysteries to one another. How else could it be, when the self – 'the varieties of ourselves' – is the long, baffling accretion of years spent on earth? The tragicomedy of misunderstanding is strongest here, for in turn Lisa knows nothing of Claudia's great love Tom, a young tank officer who met his fate in the Western Desert. 'Very likely she has never loved anyone,' thinks Lisa.

And so we ripple-dissolve to wartime Egypt, where thirtyish Claudia is keen to prove she can do a man's job, reporting from the front line for a newspaper and then kicking her heels in the unreal society of cosmopolitan Cairo, its jolly parties, swimming-pools and drinks on the terrace a world away from the searing heat and peril of the desert. At night, in 'the hot insect-rasping darkness', a green coil known as a Moon Tiger burns away to ash, repelling mosquitoes and measuring out the narrow time Tom and Claudia have together.

Penelope Lively (b.1933) spent her childhood in Cairo and acquired intimate knowledge of its sights and sounds, its babble of languages and mongrel textures. Her writing here is saturated in colour, brilliant and eye-poppingly intense as the lovers watch the line of hills on the far side of the Nile 'go from pink to amber and the water turn a sapphire blue', in contrast with the ominous colours of the desert where 'a silver glitter of tracer fire' or a 'jewelled explosion of Very lights' crests the horizon. And more in monochrome: 'Burned-out vehicles stream grey in the wind, the sky-line erupts with white puffs, a black column towers away to their right where captured enemy ammunition has been blown up.'

So vivid is the conjuring of landscape that *Moon Tiger* is likely to be recalled as a novel of place – 'the one about Egypt' – and yet it also comprises a novel of ideas, principally about the distortions and elisions of history. It celebrates marginal heroes like the Victorian civil engineer William Smith, whose canal excavations through rock highlighted the significance of stratification, and John Aubrey, who as well as writing *Brief Lives* was a pioneering archaeologist. On her hospital bed Claudia ponders her professional research into the Pilgrim Fathers, the ancient, vanished city of Memphis, Cortez and Montezuma; and then considers the way history again broke upon her own life in the form of Laszlo, a refugee from the Soviet invasion of Hungary in 1956. We are at the mercy of chaos: our understanding of what has gone before can only be elliptical, fragmentary, partial, reflecting the principle on which Lively has put together this jagged mosaic of a narrative.

As a historian Claudia has courted offence, mainly for being popular, but it's in her swagger and self-awareness that she becomes winning. (She would probably have called her memoir *I, Claudia*.) History in Lively's fiction is a subject deserving of profound respect; historians, much less so. They tend towards the pompous (Henry

Peters in *How It All Began*), the selfishly aloof (Charles in *Family Album*), the self-important (Glyn in *The Photograph*). Perhaps the slimiest exemplar is Maurice in her 1996 novel *Heatwave* – one of her very best – who writes glib, TV-friendly books about the making of myths. Appropriately enough he's also an unfaithful husband whose lies to his wife will receive a shocking comeuppance. The character of the slick opportunist, a favourite of Lively's, is embodied in *Moon Tiger* by Jasper, the spoilt, egotistical lover who gave Claudia a child and very little else. (Q. D. Leavis once made the point that the name 'Jasper' in British fiction usually signifies a cad.) The more complicated figure in Claudia's life is her brother Gordon; their close, rivalrous relationship – 'he was my sense of identity, my mirror, my critic' – shades towards incestuous love. It is the single dramatic sidelight in the book that I found less than convincing.

Thirty-four years on *Moon Tiger* feels a weightier, more intricate novel than I remembered. My admiration for it has deepened, as has my awe at the accomplishment of those closing pages. They constitute a brief front-line diary that evokes so much of the horror of war and, in the mind of one man fighting it, the pathos of duty and endurance and longing. It becomes, at moments, a kind of prayer flung out into the darkness, to his lover waiting back in Cairo:

> May she be tolerant and understanding, may she perceive the extravagance into which one is pitched by war, the suspension of ordinary common sense except that aspect of common sense needed for doing what has to be done, for telling other people what to do, for moving a lot of heavy metal around and trying to kill people with it while avoiding being killed oneself. May we, eventually, contemplate all this together.

ANTHONY QUINN's new novel *Molly & the Captain*, about a lost painting and three generations of artists, was published in 2022.

The Benefits of Writing a Biography

FRANCES DONNELLY

There are writers I particularly love because they've guided me through adult life and helped me make sense of it. Alison Lurie, who died in 2020 at the age of 94, is one such and I owe her a debt of gratitude for elegantly and slyly interpreting the seismic cultural changes that occurred in Western life from the 1960s onwards. A Radcliffe scholar, she married early and had three children, but she didn't let two rejected novels deter her, nor the husband who said: 'Perhaps it's for the best – you can spend more time with the children.'

She persevered. Her first published novel was *Love and Friendship* (1967), which is also the title of Jane Austen's first completed novel (written when Jane was 14). Like the incomparable Jane, her chief aim was 'a desire to laugh at life' through the literary medium of witty and astute comedies of manners. And like Jane she enjoyed the company of men.

Unlike Polly Alter, the feminist heroine of *The Truth about Lorin Jones* (1989). The book's opening statement is unambiguous: 'Polly Alter liked men but she wasn't sure if she trusted them anymore.' At 39, Polly is a would-be artist and recently divorced. She has taken a sabbatical from her job as an art curator in New York to write a

---

Alison Lurie, *The Truth about Lorin Jones* (1989) and *Truth and Consequences* (2005), are both out of print, but we can obtain second-hand copies.

biography of Lorin Jones, a brilliant woman artist who died early, apparently let down by the men in her life and unappreciated by the art establishment.

Subject and biographer are a good fit as Polly is in a towering fury about the way the patriarchy diminishes and controls women's lives. Take Tom, her former husband. Although hitherto a sympathetic and supportive partner, nonetheless, when offered a career-changing job in Denver he made a unilateral decision and accepted it without her agreement. Divorce follows, leaving Polly a lonely woman with the custody of Steve, her beloved 12-year-old whose upbringing has been heavy on gender-neutral toys. But Polly knows her anger towards men has an older source. The only child of a failed, young marriage, she blames her father profoundly for being such a lacklustre and absent parent.

Polly is warmly supported in her negative views by her best friend Jeanne, a radical feminist and lesbian. Jeanne has chosen to live in a world entirely populated by women. Only with their own sex, she feels, can women find respect, support and sexual fulfilment. Polly wonders if this may be her own future.

Which brings its own particular problems as Polly begins to research her book. Most of the people she'll be interviewing are the men who let Lorin down. She wants to get the best interview she can, she tells Jeanne, but how can she confront them whilst not antagonizing them?

Jeanne does not believe in confrontation at all: in lesbian tropes she is less Hip Urban Dyke, more smiling Fifties Housewife. She favours curls, ribbons and ruffled gingham aprons. In conversation she spells out words like C-R-A-P as if inquisitive younger ears are always present. She believes Polly's interviewing technique should rely heavily on placatory statements like, 'I never thought about it that way!', or 'You may be right', while hoping the male chauvinist pigs will D-A-M-N themselves out of their own mouths. Polly is not at all sure that this disarming, non-confrontational approach is the one a modern feminist should be employing. There is something about Jeanne's method, placatory and fundamentally dishonest, that sits badly with her.

But how else is she going to discover the truth about Lorin Jones? It's hard enough to understand our own friends, let alone someone you haven't even met. A well-respected biographer, about to embark without much pleasure on a new subject, once confided to me that writing a biography, like bereavement, fell into four stages.

Stage One was passionate over-identification with the subject. Stage Two was panic at the tsunami of conflicting material gathered. Stage Three was an actual dislike of your subject and a profound wish you'd chosen someone else. Stage Four was a glum acceptance that it's impossible to know another human being. You can only present all the material in an unbiased way and let readers make up their own minds.

These jaundiced observations certainly resemble Polly's own journey to discover the truth about Lorin Jones. Her over-identification with her subject is apparent. But as the interviews stack up, the picture that emerges is complicated and not always flattering. The two certainties are that Lorin was beautiful and talented. Less attractive is the realization that she employed her beauty to facilitate her talent. When it came to making use of other people – usually men – Lorin could teach a master class. Her looks reeled them in, but once they were in place and taking care of her she absented herself mentally to get on with her painting.

This is a damning indictment until one considers that this may be what male geniuses have always done. They've traditionally enjoyed the services of an uncomplaining someone who'll have dinner on the table. Often this person is called A Wife. So should we really look askance at a woman artist who needs the same conditions to nurture her own talent?

This is clearly an issue of interest to Alison Lurie who returns to it again in *Truth and Consequences* (2005). In this book we meet Delia

Delaney, a minor literary celebrity and writer of darkly Gothic tales, usually referred to as 'The American Angela Carter'. Delia is an almost cartoonish character, a siren with white bosoms and tumbled Titian hair. But the gorgeous physical attributes conceal a steely will. She makes use of everyone in a breathless, seductive and completely unapologetic way. Yet at the same time she utters some profound truths about the problem of trying to clear a space in which to create. Everyone, she says in justification, wants a piece of you. Everyone has an unpublished novel in their bedside drawer that they want you to read. To make your own space, you have to be ruthless. Lorin Jones would be nodding her beautiful head in emphatic agreement.

Predictably, Polly reaches the Fourth Stage of Biography over-whelmed as to how to present Lorin's story. Yes, Lorin Jones was a brilliant artist. But she damaged people and had a profoundly self-destructive streak. This has to be balanced against the fact that everyone interviewed had their own agenda and wanted to come out of the book looking good. How can all this contradictory evidence be presented fairly?

Polly's confusion is compounded by the fact that she has fallen in love with one of Lorin's ex-partners, the very attractive Hugh Cameron, who lives in Key West. The lesbian sisterhood suddenly looks a whole lot less appealing and Polly and Jeanne have a fatal quarrel.

Alone in her apartment the day after Christmas, paralysed as to how to start her book, Polly finds herself facing a few unpalatable truths about her own life. Could it be she's played some part in the way men have treated her? She's uncomfortably aware that, looking back, her father had actually made strenuous efforts to keep in touch with a very cross little daughter. And her husband, contrary to the way she'd been telling the story, had bent over backwards to accom-modate her needs in the proposed move to Denver. She had refused point blank to even consider it.

In this new mood of self-awareness she's able to ask herself, grievances aside, what is it she really wants? If her book is a success she can have a career in the New York art world – a slightly bleak kind of success. It would be a future of affairs with 'people whom she doesn't really like or trust and who don't much like or trust her'. The alternative is leaving New York with her son for Key West, putting her faith (again!) in one man, writing her book and starting again as an artist.

When *Truth and Consequences* was published it attracted some hostility from the Radical Feminists who felt they'd been unfairly represented. But the book makes clear that what actually interests Alison Lurie is less sexual politics than the tensions within any group who claim to have created Utopia. Living on the moral high ground is both fraught and exhausting. What starts with the search for ideological truth so often ends in meltdown about who didn't do the dishes. Selfishness, the Old Adam – or Eve in this case – always manifests itself. The examination of this behaviour – the dichotomy between what you claim to think and what you actually do – is of the keenest interest to both Alison Lurie and Jane Austen. And it's what makes both these books so wonderfully entertaining.

FRANCES DONNELLY lives on the Norfolk/Suffolk border, and is still in search of a rescue dog. Ideally small and easy-going, a GSOH essential.

In Johnson's Footsteps

NIGEL ANDREW

'We're thinking of moving,' announced our son one evening last year. 'To Lichfield.' Lichfield! The name was music to my ears. I have long had a soft spot for that little gem of a cathedral city, once the ecclesiastical capital of Mercia, now a delightful Staffordshire market town. I would be more than happy to follow the son, daughter-in-law and three of the grandchildren to Lichfield (and my wife, less familiar with Lichfield, would follow them wherever they went anyway).

They went, we followed, and now here we are, settling into life in a place very different from the south London suburb that was our previous home. Why was I so keen to move here? The cathedral of course, with its three graceful spires rising over the waters of the Minster Pool, and the streets of Georgian brick and stone interspersed with half-timbering, the wonderful parks and open spaces, the gentle pace of life, the friendly openness of the people . . . And one very special reason: the evident pride the town takes in its most famous native son – Samuel Johnson.

For years I have enjoyed Johnson's writings – the *Rambler* essays, his life of Richard Savage, *The Vanity of Human Wishes*, even the great *Dictionary* – and, thanks to James Boswell's extraordinary *Life*, surely the most rounded and affectionate biography ever written, I have also loved him as a man, for all his faults. He could be overbearing, pompous and opinionated, yet he was also tender-hearted, affectionate, sympathetic and well aware of his own shortcomings. To live in the town where he was born and spent his formative years was a pleasing prospect, especially as he is still so very present there.

Johnson, who once opined that 'Every man has a lurking wish to appear considerable in his native place', would be gratified to see that he still appears very considerable in Lichfield, where he was born in 1709. The city signs proudly declare Lichfield the 'Birthplace of Samuel Johnson', his statue stands in the marketplace and, remarkably, his birthplace, which was his father's bookshop, survives, and is now a Johnson museum – and bookshop. There is even a Samuel Johnson Community Hospital – which would have pleased him, as he took a lively interest in 'physic' and his father had a sideline in selling patent medicines.

The Johnson statue looms large in the marketplace. Atop a tall plinth decorated with scenes from his Lichfield years, Johnson sits brooding, chin on fist, in a throne-like chair. When the statue was unveiled in 1838, it was regarded by some as insufficiently heroic in style, but it conveys the introspective, melancholic aspect of Johnson's personality rather well. Anyway, it is nicely offset by the statue at the other end of the marketplace – a jaunty figure, on a smaller scale, of (who else but?) Boswell. The birthplace museum, also on the marketplace, is a pleasing mix of original and reconstructed interiors, with steep narrow staircases and small rooms with creaking floors, displaying various items of Johnsoniana, including the famous Nollekens bust, many books and pictures, and some of Johnson's furniture and effects. And the second-hand bookshop downstairs is excellent.

One of the rooms of the museum is the one in which Johnson was born. 'My mother had a very difficult and dangerous labour,' he wrote in a posthumously published memoir. 'I was born almost dead, and could not cry for some time. When [the male midwife] had me in his arms, he said, "Here is a brave boy."' Johnson's father was that year Sheriff of Lichfield, and due to ride the Circuit of the County, a ceremonial occasion of great pomp. To celebrate his son's birth, 'he feasted the citizens with uncommon magnificence'.

Soon after this, the baby Samuel was, 'by my father's persuasion', put out to a wet-nurse. Clearly his mother was not happy with this arrangement:

My mother visited me every day, and used to go different ways, that her assiduity might not expose her to ridicule; and often left her fan or glove behind her, that she might have a pretence to come back unexpected; but she never discovered any token of neglect. Dr Swinfen [a young doctor lodging with the Johnsons at the time of Samuel's birth] told me, that the scrofulous sores which afflicted me proceeded from the bad humours of the nurse, whose son had the same distemper, and was likewise short-sighted, but in a less degree. My mother thought my diseases derived from her family. In ten weeks I was taken home, a poor, diseased infant, almost blind.

As well as the scrofula detected by Dr Swinfen – which left Johnson scarred and visually impaired for life – he later developed an alarming range of tics and twitches that might well have been a form of Tourette's. He was also, from his youth, dogged by what we would now call depression.

His was not a promising start in life, and his family circumstances were far from ideal. Johnson senior was a hopeless businessman who never thought to keep any kind of accounts, and as a result was perpetually in chronic financial difficulty. When asked in later life why he said little about his early years, Johnson replied, 'One has so little pleasure in reciting the anecdotes of beggary' – an exaggeration, but certainly the young Johnson lived in straitened circumstances. Although he was a brilliant scholar, the star pupil of Lichfield Grammar School, he was only able to take up a place at Pembroke College, Oxford, because of a timely bequest by an aunt. And even then, he had to return home after a little over a year, the money having run out. Several unhappy years followed, in which Johnson, trying to find a way ahead, became a schoolteacher, a job for which he was woefully unsuited.

His great good fortune was to find love with Elizabeth Porter, the widow of a friend, who, though twenty-one years his senior, was happy to marry this impoverished young man, and was to be the love of his life, his 'Tetty', whose loss (she died in 1752) grieved him for the rest of his days. Elizabeth was a woman of property, and with the help of her capital, she and Johnson set up a school at Edial Hall, near Lichfield. Sadly it was a failure, never attracting more than a handful of pupils, but one of them was David Garrick, also an alumnus of Lichfield Grammar School, and later to be the most celebrated actor of his day. He and Johnson became firm friends and, when the school failed in 1737, they decided their best course would be to make their way to London in search of fame and fortune. Elizabeth would follow in due course, when Johnson had found his feet.

It was a struggle, in the course of which Johnson saw much of the seamy side of London life and the lower depths of the literary world, the Grub Street of desperate hacks and dubious dealings – but his talent, as poet, essayist, biographer and novelist (*Rasselas, Prince of Abissinia*), won through, and he was soon embarked on what was to be a brilliant, if arduous, career. His future was clearly going to be in London, not Lichfield, where the literary scene was very much more limited. There, only one star shone brightly – Erasmus Darwin, grandfather of Charles and himself a pioneer of evolutionary theory.

Erasmus Darwin was a polymath – physician, naturalist, philosopher, inventor and poet – who presented his scientific findings to the world in (rather bad) verse, and was a leading light of the Lunar Society, an affiliation of scientists, philosophers, writers, engineers and businessmen that was at the heart of what we now call the Midlands Enlightenment. But that is another story (for which see Jenny Uglow's excellent *The Lunar Men*) and one in which Johnson, as only an occasional visitor to Lichfield, played little or no part. On the few occasions when Johnson and Darwin, men of equally huge physique and presence, met, 'mutual and strong dislike subsisted between them', according to Anna Seward, the 'Swan of Lichfield', poetess and queen bee of the city's literati. The touchy Seward declared that she could not forgive Johnson his 'many hints of

Lichfield's intellectual barrenness'. But did he really make such remarks, or did the Swan of Lichfield resent the great man's pardonable reluctance to meet her, despite Boswell's efforts to bring such a meeting about?

At other times Johnson was certainly happy to sing the virtues of his native city, describing it as 'a city of philosophers', and on one occasion relating how 'I lately took my friend Boswell and showed him genuine civilized life in an English provincial town.' Lichfield is even honoured with a mention in Johnson's *Dictionary*, under his definition of 'lich' ('a dead carcase'): 'Lichfield, the field of the dead, a city in Staffordshire, so named from martyred Christians. *Salve magna parens* [Hail, great parent].'

Towards the end of his life, Johnson ensured that his parents were remembered with a suitably dignified stone slab, inscribed with a long Latin epitaph written by their son, in the floor of St Michael's church in Lichfield (where another pair of literary parents – Philip Larkin's – are buried in the graveyard). Johnson certainly loved London and he could hardly have pursued his particular career anywhere else but it is clear, too, that the city of his birth always had a place in his heart, and Lichfield, happily, seems to feel much the same way about him. Johnson famously said that 'When a man is tired of London, he is tired of life.' I would update that to 'When a man is tired of London [as increasing numbers are], he should seriously consider moving to Lichfield.'

NIGEL ANDREW is the author of *The Mother of Beauty: On the Golden Age of English Church Monuments, and Other Matters of Life and Death*. He writes the largely literary blog 'Nigeness: A Hedonic Resource' and has been working an unconscionably long time on a book about butterflies.

Bibliography

Coming attractions

MARTIN SORRELL catches up with a murderer · OLIVIA POTTS goes back to basics · TIM PEARS is impressed by a long Life · SARAH WEDDERBURN meets an unusual therapist · JIM RING revisits Colditz · KATE YOUNG is unnerved by Shirley Hazard · JONATHAN LAW takes a fresh look at the landscape · SUE GEE finds inspiration in a bookmark · WILLIAM PALMER gets involved in the American Civil War